CARING FOR
PARENTS
AND OTHER
LOVED ONES

MORE PRAISE FOR

Caring for Parents and Other Loved Ones

"Written with love and compassion, the step-by-step resources in this book are vital tools for handling the final care of a loved one, as well as your own grief and loss. The ancestors, saints, and sages are celebrating—the well-done dance continues."

—Earl L. Gardner, Founder of Agape Spirit Foundation and licensed Therapist with 30 years' experience working with Veterans in Los Angeles, California

"All of us, at some point in our lives, will find ourselves caring for someone we love deeply, who is very ill and who may be dying. ... Wilson Simmons' book, *Caring for Parents and Other Loved Ones*... offers a valuable roadmap through the rocky emotional terrain as well as the mountain of medical information and practical necessities that face us daily when a loved one needs our help."

—Mignon McCarthy, Author, Editor

CARING FOR
PARENTS
AND OTHER
LOVED ONES

A Guide for the 21st Century

Foreword by
Michael Bernard Beckwith, Author of *Life Visioning*
Founder, Agape International Spiritual Center

WILSON SIMMONS III

author of award-winning, *Inside Corporate America, A Guide for African Americans*

ARPress
ILLUMINATING IDEAS
EMPOWERING VOICES

ARPress
45 Dan Road Suite 36
Canton MA 02021

| Hotline: | 1(888) 821-0229 |
| Fax: | 1(508) 545-7580 |

Ordering Information:
Quantity Sales. Special discounts are available on quantity purchases by corporations, associations, and others. For details, contact the publisher at the address above.

Printed in the United States of America.

| ISBN-13 | Paperback | 979-8-89389-068-6 |
| | eBook | 979-8-89389-069-3 |

Library of Congress Control Number: 2024914273

Dedicated to the memory of

Cecellia Jean Simmons

Contents

ACKNOWLEDGMENTS

Special gratitude and love to my two ANGELS: Eboni Simret Wright and Sarah Presley. It is easy to see why God sent you to help me, guide me on the journey, lift me when I fall, and nudge me when I need it most.

I am grateful to my family and friends who have shared personal experiences, encouraged me, and lifted my spirits. Thank you: Judge Dixon, Donna King, Saman Wright, Joe Louis, Leann Niess, Sydney M. Lee, Larry Williams, Lloyd Ferguson, Calvin Sweeney, Clinton Woods, Harold Logwood, Anzecus, Omega Psi Phi Fraternity, Delta Sigma Theta Sorority, Maya Zuri Louis, Mary J. Goodbeer, Sabine Fimbres, Siri Vhed Khalsa, Rose LaFrance, Melvin Bell, Bertram Bell and Chickee Nelson.

FOREWORD

I begin the Foreword to this remarkable book by thanking the spirit of Wilson Simmons III's mother, Mary Jacquet Simmons, for cultivating within him the quality of unconditional love, the compassion of a Buddha's heart, and the courage of a spiritual warrior. Caressed as it is with wisdom and practicality, Wilson's journey is very personal to me where the precious memory of my own beloved mother, Alice G. Beckwith, is concerned. It is from direct experience that I say regardless of whether you are caretaking a loved one, if you are sharing the responsibility with other family members, if your loved one is in a care facility, or if you are reading this book on your own behalf, you will find in these pages the full spectrum of how you may skillfully navigate the position in which you find yourself and/or them.

First and foremost, it should be understood that this book is not only for a time of imminent crisis where we or a loved one are concerned. In our Western society where aging, illness, the process of dying and death itself are, in general, related to with a denial mentality, a book like *Caring for Parents and Other Loved Ones* is vital to our life-education. Simmons' guidance addresses many vital issues such as shifts in physical prowess, senior driving skills, discerning mental skills, along with holistic approaches to the countless details in caring for an elderly, ill, or dying loved one.

And with the utmost respect and love, he includes the spiritual aspects of this intimate and profound journey that awaits us all.

From the birth of the hospice movement in 1948 by physician Dame Cicely Saunders, who began her work with the terminally ill in a suburb of London at St. Christopher's Hospice, to 1972 when Dr. Elisabeth Kubler-Ross presented to the world her classic bestseller, *On Death and Dying*, encouraging progress has been made. As Kubler-Ross wrote, "We live in a very particular deathdenying society. We isolate both the dying and the old, and it serves a purpose. They are reminders of our own mortality." As we celebrate 40 years of hospice care in the US and a healthy shift in our long-held attitudes and practices, the book you hold in your hands is a most valuable resource. Simmons gives us all new eyes with which to view and relate to what living has to do with dying, and what dying has to do with living.

Whether you are the patient, a loved one, the caregiver or both, this book offers the encouragement, trust, compassion, solace, and skillful means to walk the path with confidence. It is a gift to us all, and I highly encourage you to share it with family members, friends, and any caregivers you know.

Michael Bernard Beckwith
Author of *Life Visioning*
Founder, Agape International Spiritual Center

INTRODUCTION

"There are only four kinds of people in this world: those who have been caregivers, those who currently are caregivers, those who will be caregivers, and those who will need caregivers."

— ROSALYN CARTER, former First Lady, wife of President Jimmy Carter

THIS BOOK WILL empower senior citizens and their caregivers by bringing a bright light, as well as viable solutions, to a condition in our society that has been cast into a dark corner. Healthcare for seniors in the United States is encumbered by bureaucracy, apathetic policymakers, a corrupt Medicare/Medicaid system, and hospital conglomerates designed almost exclusively for profit. To date, these systems and our government are doing a poor job of serving the very people who built this country: hardworking people who believed their twilight years would mean lying in a hammock sipping cold lemonade. Instead, they are finding themselves being treated with disrespect and, in many cases, tied down to beds or wheelchairs and treated with disdain.

Many of our senior citizens feel as if they have been cast aside like yesterday's trash. Can it be that the very system to which we have been paying our share of Social Security and taxes is now earmarking those hard-earned funds for war, and worse, for bailing out the rich, good ol' boys on Wall Street, most of whom will never have to worry about healthcare or a place to live?

Seniors represent a very powerful force in modern society and our numbers continue to grow. In fact, someone turns 50 every seven seconds, and the senior population is expected to increase to more than 70 million by the year 2030. We have a responsibility to each other. Rosalyn Carter, former First Lady and wife of President Jimmy Carter, said it best: "There are only four kinds of people in this world: those who have been caregivers, those who currently are caregivers, those who will be caregivers, and those who will need caregivers." That pretty much includes all of us.

Based on studies done over the past two decades, 75% of caregivers are women, yet in the last five years, more and more men are becoming involved in caring for aging parents and loved ones. More than 55% of the caregivers in the **1988 Pines Burnout Measure (BM) Study** said that they were experiencing burnout, and 85% complained of just being plain exhausted. "Caregiver" by definition means you are going to be exhausted in the best of circumstances. The life of a caregiver becomes a marathon of tasks, hopes, and disappointments. Added to that are family members who may find fault in everything the caregiver does.

I had the honor of caring for my mother, Mary Jacquet Simmons, for the last five years of her life. As a caregiver, I covered the range of emotions—resentment, irritation, confusion, disappointment, bitterness, discontent, and distress—most of which had little to do with the actual care.

I once read an article that said the quality of a civilization is judged by how it cares for its seniors. In many countries, seniors are treasured and treated with reverence. If you are that gifted soul who cares for a parent or another loved one, embrace your own goodness. Let your loved one know how much you love them. But first and foremost, seek out the best possible care, advocate for it, and take care of yourself in the process.

Mary Jacquet Simmons—affectionately called "Mae" by friends and family and "Mom" by me—was born in St. Martinsville, Louisiana in 1915. She graduated with honors from Phyllis Wheatley High School in Houston, Texas, followed by enrollment at Southern University in Baton Rouge back in her home state. Mae then acquired a small business in Houston, where she often accompanied her famous brother, saxophonist Illinois Jacquet, on the stand-up bass.

On a quest for new horizons, Mae moved to Los Angeles just as the U.S. entered WWII. Workers were being recruited for wartime jobs, and Mae answered the call and became the first black women to work as a welder on U.S. ships built in the San Pedro Harbor for military use. Black, smart, and beautiful, Mae broke the color line and prompted even her white, male co-workers to respect her. When asked by one of her white counterparts why she wasn't home baking cookies, she replied, "Because my husband is the cook!"

Some of Mae's other achievements include ownership of her own maintenance business, teaching and then becoming Dean of Women at Emma Hughes Business College, and appointment as one of the original teachers in the Head Start Program in Los Angeles. Through all of it, Mae was active in her community, in political affairs, in service auxiliaries, and as a leader in the development and activities of Los Angeles City Councilman Nate Holden's Senior Citizen Center.

Mae would be the first to agree, however, that her most significant achievement was the rearing of six children, all of whom attended school in Compton and grew into contributing members of their own communities as adults.

A Reminder: Caregivers Age, Too!

Caring for the elderly at the age 75 is scary for yourself, which means maintaining your health as your first priority and planning for your end of life if you haven't already done so. If you are fortunate enough to still have a parent at this point in life then the same two issues apply. A person at age 75 and above will certainly have health issues that need to be addressed in the best of circumstances because age brings about changes that insist that you modify your lifestyle.

Planning for this period in your life is key to being able to live in some measure of comfort with or without assistance. In my experience, expecting a child or other relative to step in and provide the necessary assistance is not a reliable plan. I currently live in an age 55 and over community where many of the needs for people of advanced age are made available in close proximity. Things such easy access to grocery stores, medical and dental facilities, cleaning services, transportation assistance, age-appropriate exercise and recreational facilities, convenient entertainment, maid services, and other areas of assistance that people need as they advance in age.

Still, this may not be enough. As you advance in age you will need the assistance of what I will call an advocate or caretaker. Without a caretaker you will in most likelihood find yourself in an assisted living center or nursing home. The quality-of-care ranges from excellent to dangerously poor in these homes and usually, without planning for one you won't have much time to research or investigate when one is needed. The best homes usually are more expensive and have a waiting list to get in.

To further reinforce the need for planning are the financial implications of living independently and comfortably as you age. Health being first implies that you have adequate medical coverage, this is not always a given as the need for treatment almost certainly increases with age. And coverage needs to have been arranged well in advance of advanced age. The same applies to the arrangement of a caretaker, this should be arranged well in advance of the actual need because it may become a necessity with little warning, and it can be all-encompassing job.

One of the most difficult things to plan for is your own end of life, that is to say your funeral, burial and the distribution of your state. I was fortunate enough to have parents that put their own plans in place with a little prodding and persistence from me and my siblings. It has been something that I put off in my own case until recently and at age 75 can I really expect to have plenty of time to address it. I have seen the resulting dysfunction in other case where these things failed to be put in place, and they can result in hardships and painful experiences for families that are difficult to overcome. The old adage "a failure to plan is a plan to fail" when it comes to planning for your advance years is a truism that will confront all of us that are lucky to live long enough to be considered elderly

CHAPTER 1
Making the Decision to Become a Caregiver

"Whoever destroys a single life is as guilty as though he had destroyed the entire world; and whoever rescues a single life earns as much merit as though he had rescued the entire world."

— THE TALMUD

LOOKING BACK, A string of sleepless nights was a harbinger. It was 1993 and I was living in San Francisco, at Bay and Leavenworth in the Fisherman's Wharf district. Alcatraz stood a mile offshore, a bracing daily caution to do the right thing or else. But I had no worries of that kind, or any other, at the time. Life was good. I just wasn't sleeping. I didn't know why. Ordinarily, the nighttime sounds of the city, even the clanking of the cable cars on Bay Street, escorted me into deep sleep. But not now. Easy sleep eluded me. I tossed and turned until the alarm went off at 6:30 every morning. And during the day, I felt unsettled, restless, cranky, agitated, impatient, and fidgety.

Only once before in my life had I been this wired and strung out. It was 1968 and I was preparing to leave the Oakland Army Base to fly to Vietnam. Back then, the reason for my discomfort was clear and present danger. This time, twenty-five years later, I had no clue, which was more than disconcerting. It drained me.

The second week of this crazy insomnia was playing itself out when a simple phone call led to another simple phone that then took a sharp, unexpected left-turn into a family situation that quickly brought things into focus. My cousin Willa called me at my office with the news that she'd been downsized by her company and with questions about how to roll over her retirement fund without paying penalties. I phoned my close friend Judge Dixon immediately, an executive with IBM in Los Angeles. As I expected, Judge—his first name, not his occupation—had all the answers Willa would need. He shrugged off my thanks in his usual manner and said, "No big deal." After a pause, he said softly, "Did you know that your mother is in a nursing home?"

I went numb. After a long silence, I could only mutter, "What? Where?"

"A place called Alcott Center on Pico Boulevard here in Los Angeles, I think," he answered in a measured tone, entering respectfully into a family matter not his own. But Judge and I had more than 40 years of friendship behind us. He knew that what he was saying had to be said.

I thanked him and hung up the phone, angry, confused and extremely hurt. I had been under the impression that Mom was being taken care of by my three older sisters, Theresa, Stephanie, and Maggie. The four of us had agreed on this plan months ago, before I moved to Northern California, a plan arranged with the help of both Mom's nurse and therapist. I had taken care of Mom for two years, and my sisters were now to alternate her care for a year, making this a "family project." What the hell happened?

I called Mom's home first, still in disbelief. The answering machine told me to leave a message. I tried one of my sister's numbers and got no answer. I called Dr. Mary Taylor, Mom's doctor, and she was also unavailable. Quickly I dialed airline reservations, made plans to fly out of San Francisco first thing in next morning, and then called Judge, who was waiting for me curbside as I dashed out of the LAX terminal the next day.

We didn't say much to each other as Judge drove me to the Alcott Nursing Home and dropped me off. I dragged my luggage into the foyer, marched up to the front desk and demanded, "Who's in charge?" I was given a man's name and told he was busy. I let the lady at the front desk know that I was there to take my mother out of the nursing home.

The receptionist informed me that Alcott is not only a nursing home but also a rehabilitation center, to which I responded, "Whatever!" I was not angry and kept my voice measured. I didn't want to appear intimidating, yet I cut the woman off in mid-sentence, asking to see my mother immediately. A nurse was instructed to take me to her room.

Mom was eating her breakfast. When she looked up and saw me, she squealed with excitement, causing the eggs to fly out of her mouth. "My big son, my baby!" she yelled, dropping her spoon to extend her arms. I whispered in her ear, "I'm here to take you home, Mama." She didn't reply, yet the wide grin on her face said it all. Mom could hardly contain herself. I looked into her eyes and explained that I still had some unfinished business to take care of, then I left her with a gigantic smile on her face.

Back to the front desk, before I could say a word, the head nurse told me that Dr. Taylor had been notified and that, should I take my mother from the premises, it would be without her approval. I listened intently and said, "When will the director be available?" Ignoring my question, the nurse continued on about Center policy. Just then the director appeared—a tall, lean, and well-dressed man with an air about him that said, "I run this joint." He motioned for me to follow him, which I did, his slow pace down the hall maddening. But anything short of jogging was too slow for me at this point. Finally reaching his office, he offered me a seat as he appropriated an oversized black leather chair, too big both for him and his office. He leaned back, his hands folded over his chest.

Where do I sign to take my mother out of here?" I said.

The director looked startled. He stopped rocking and sat upright.

Onto the director's desk, I put my driver's license and the paperwork naming me Mom's Power of Attorney. I identified myself as the son of Mary Jacquet Simmons, the woman in Room 324. I proceeded to hammer him with questions. Who admitted my mother? Why? When? I want him on the defensive. I want him as upset with this situation as I am and will not be satisfied until his fists are clenched.

He told me that Mom's physician, Dr. Taylor, and my sisters think it best to have Mom rehabilitated in the center for the next three months. I asked the director to take a good look at the paperwork I just put before him, to note that I have Power of Attorney and am the only one with the authority to make that decision.

No longer did he have the look of the confident director. His voice trailed off as he searched for a comeback and mumbled inanities about the Center's outstanding staff. I backed off and offered the voice of reason. I told him that I understood the difficulty of his job in dealing with the families of residents. I even apologized for the misunderstanding in my own family's case. Calm restored, I asked for the papers for my mother's release.

The phone beeped just then. Dr. Taylor was calling to give the okay to Alcott to release my mother. After excusing himself, the director returned with the necessary papers for my signature. Everything was all of a sudden falling nicely into place.

We shook hands. I sat down in lobby to wait for Mom. The front-desk staff whispered among themselves, easy for me to ignore. A half-hour later Mom was wheeled out. Her face was glowing. I felt heroic for the very first time in my life.

IN SUMMARY

Regardless of how the decision is made to care for a parent or loved one, and whether that decision is a choice or a necessity, prepare to feel a range of emotions from hero to martyr. Being a caregiver is a gift from God. Embrace it. The fact is, if you have Medicare alone it covers only short periods of skilled nursing home care after a hospital stay.

WISE TIPS

Prayer, soft words, big hugs, and being close enough for your parent to know that he or she is loved. To Mom, I read the Bible, poetry, and funny stories. I played her favorite music—Illinois Jacquet, Nina Simone, Ella Fitzgerald, and Sara Vaughn. Music put Mom in a positive state.

CAREGIVING QUOTES

I have resided in a senior residence for the past two and a half years. I love living in my present location. I feel safe and secure, and despite the fact that I am alone, I am not lonely. There is beauty all around. I have a beautiful view of Lake Michigan, which when viewed early in the morning, seems spiritually serene and calming.

Do I long to go back? No, I just say to myself that it was God who brought me safe thus far and God will lead me on. I am where He wants me to be at this time, in a wonderful senior residence and not a nursing home. The average age here is 80 and many of the residents require the use of wheelchairs, walkers, canes, etc. I currently have a walker and oxygen, but I did not have the oxygen when I came here. Sometimes it is depressing to watch people deteriorate right before your very eyes and, yes, several have passed away; including four who had become my friends.

— ELIZABETH WILKS, 85, Chicago, Ill

"It is not your obligation to complete your work,
but you are not at liberty to quit."
— THE TALMUD —

CHAPTER 2
Daily Challenges for the Full Time Caregiver

The challenge is in the moment, the time is always now."
— JAMES BALDWIN

AFTER LEAVING THE nursing home with Mom alongside me, we arrived at my home without incident. As we walked in the door of my apartment, I suddenly realized that before me lay the heavy responsibility for Mom's care. Preceding Mom's recent stay in the nursing home and before she went into the hospital, she could do most everything herself. She could be forgetful, but she was pretty self-reliant. After all, she had raised six children, some of whom were not her own. She belonged to two churches, was president of the PTA, and was supervising teacher for Head Start.

But now, things had changed. Once I became Mom's caregiver, I was determined to get her the right foods, understand what medications she was taking, and contact key health care providers, which included doctors, a physical therapist, an occupational therapist, and a speech therapist. My first goal, however, was to set up the house so it was senior-friendly.

ENVIRONMENT

Since a great deal of my mother's time would be spent in her bedroom, I wanted it to be as safe, comfortable, and functional as possible. Clutter throughout the house had to be removed, which would help to prevent falls and other accidents. It should be easy for her to move around in every room and things should be especially easy to locate. I also arranged her closet so Mom would be able to find the simple things she needed on a daily basis, including her pajamas, robe, and daytime clothes. I substituted hooks for hangers to make it easier.

Next, I put a nightstand beside her bed with a phone and a list of numbers for doctors, family members, and friends. The table was large enough to accommodate a pillbox for medications taken at night or upon waking, water, and a TV remote. I included a family picture as well as a bell on Mom's nightstand, which took very little energy to ring if she needed to signal me. An intercom or two-way baby monitor would also work for this purpose.

Lighting in the room, as well as throughout the house, needed to be adjusted to suit Mom's needs. It had to be bright enough for reading magazines, newspapers, and books next to her bed. Lights in the hallway leading to the bathroom and other passageways also needed to be bright enough for her to find her way during the night. I knew I needed to eliminate possible falls, since I'd learned that half of seniors who break or fracture their hips become permanently disabled, and as many as 25% die within a year.

I had this conversation with my mother almost daily, "Watch your step, Mom! Hold on to the handrails, Baby!" She fell a few times; most seniors do. When we would have the talk, I would say to Mom that if she broke her hip, I would no longer be able to help her. She would probably have to end up in a facility that specializes in caring for seniors who are unable to walk. She understood, but when you've been independent for most of your life, sometimes the words don't really resonate.

To help prevent falls, I also installed grab bars in the bathroom. They are easy to install and are helpful for balance of seniors in general. Grab bars or handrails along the hallway are sometimes necessary to navigate a solo walk.

I got a large-faced clock to mount on the wall and a large calendar to keep track of the day and time of upcoming medical appointments, family visits, leisure activities, and so on. Mom was prone to minor strokes, known as Transient Ischemic Attacks (TIAs). As the strokes became more frequent, she would ask me what day it was—one of a series of questions that the doctor would ask her—and she wanted to have the dates and numbers memorized before she went in to be examined. The calendar would bring her pretty close to answering most of the questions. Mom loved it as though she were preparing to take an exam for a class.

There were a number of other, smaller things I did to make Mom's room more comfortable. I placed a big, comfortable reclining chair for her to sit in, while she relaxed watching TV, reading poetry or interesting articles, and listening to music. My mother loved poetry—that, and hearing the sound of her baby brother, Illinois Jacquet, blow his saxophone. Nothing brought a bigger smile to her face. Having a chair in the room also ensured Mom got out of bed regularly. She got into the routine of walking to her chair, and I encouraged her to walk, even with her walker, for as long as she could each day, since being active is critical to longevity.

I also incorporated as many of Mom's personal possessions into her room as possible. We hung her pictures on the walls and brought in plants and flowers that she was fond of. My sister Stephanie would always bring flowers whenever she was in town. They made a big difference in the room and cheered Mom immensely.

I purchased Mom an adjustable hospital bed with the side gates through Medicare. The gates would prevent her from falling out. They also prevented her from trying to get up on her own to go to the bathroom unassisted. It finally occurred to me to also put a portable toilet next to Mom's bed, so at night she could step right out of the bed and relieve herself. It made all the difference in the world.

Here is a general checklist of what should be done throughout the house for overall safety:

- Remove all throw rugs (or tape them down)
- Remove electrical cords from the floor and tape them to the wall
- Install bright (100-watt bulb) lighting in the house
- Install grab bars and/or handrails throughout the house, including the bathroom
- Place non-skid strips on the bathroom floor and bathtub
- Purchase a shower seat for your loved one's comfort and ease
- Install an adjustable shower head with a handle
- Install a toilet seat with handles on the sides that can be gripped for support

- Install air conditioning if you live in a humid climate (fans won't cut it)
- Install a ramp for a wheel chair if you have steps
- Keep a night light on in the bathroom
- Remove locks from bathroom and bedroom doors
- Keep a sturdy step stool with handrails in the kitchen
- Arrange storage of goods at waist level
- Lower cabinet shelves
- Clean spills as soon as they happen
- Remove all breakable items
- Keep frequently used kitchen items readily accessible (toaster, can opener, coffeemaker, etc.)
- Remove low tables, footrests and other items from pathways
- Arrange furniture to create a pathway between rooms
- Remove everything from the stairs
- Install sturdy handrails in stairways, even if there's only one step.
- Apply non-slip treads to steps and bare floors to ensure proper footing

After making the house senior-friendly, the next focus was Mom's diet and then her medications.

APPETITE

Once I took over as Mom's full-time caregiver, I changed her diet quite a bit. I believe in the importance of diet and exercise, as discussed in the following chapter in detail, but for Mom, eating the proper foods, as well as eating at all, became an immediate issue.

First of all, with all of the medications she was taking, constipation became an issue. Also, Mom loved fried foods and all the stuff that clogs the intestines. Her doctors recommended that she take a laxative to soften her stool; instead, I began giving her fruit in the morning, and alternating that with oatmeal. At a family gathering, Mom told everyone within earshot, "My son is feeding me mush!" Salads and vegetables were not a big hit with her either. The very foods that she gave me as a child were now the ones she found unappetizing. Her roots, after all, were in St. Martinville, Louisiana.

Mom's appetite continued to decrease, and she became increasingly irritable. I found myself bribing her with going to Mass on Sunday if she would just eat. It was a strange contrast to the way she had spent most of her life. She was normally overweight, which used to worry me to no end. Yet now, I could hardly get her to eat.

Dehydration was another challenge for us at first. Even before I could get our living arrangements completely organized, Mom landed back in the hospital. Of course, there were members of my family saying, in no uncertain terms, that Mom should be admitted back into the nursing home. I felt otherwise, but the fact still remained that Mom had to go back to the hospital, because she was dehydrated. She was hooked up to an IV and given lots of fluids. After a couple of days, she was back at home.

As I discussed Mom's condition with Dr. Taylor, she explained how important it was for me to be patient. Mom had to drink more water, but I started with trying to give her a cup of water, and then moved onto a straw, but it was still difficult to get Mom to drink a lot without her gagging. I called Dr. Taylor once again for advice and she told me, "Wilson, you have to be patient." I said, "Patient, what do you mean?" She said emphatically, "Give your mother water with a spoon, if necessary." I finally got it. Dr. Taylor was talking about being patient. I was talking about giving Mom water. Giving Mom water was going to take patience on my part. I had to remind myself: Do you run out of patience when your child is learning to walk? Do you stop assisting if they don't walk after a year? Where do you draw the line? The truth is that there is no line. You will work with your baby until they walk. Mom was now my "baby," and I had to exercise all the patience I could with her. At first it took almost a half-hour for Mom to drink the equivalent of a glass of water, but as I became more proficient, she got better. She was healing and was soon able to use a straw to drink.

MEDICATION

The medication that Dr. Taylor prescribed for Mom was paid for by Medicare most of the time, but the ones that weren't covered were expensive. Fortunately, it was an infrequent occurrence. As I met more people dealing with the issue of having to pay out-of-pocket for different medications, it became clear that drug companies were taking full advantage of the American system of mark-up.

To date, quite a few people I know are buying their medicine from Canada. There are groups of seniors going by the busload to Canada to fill their prescriptions. Since this phenomenon is becoming more widespread, one must wonder what the drug companies are paying the government to make it illegal to buy medication outside of the U.S.

China is the largest manufacturer of toys, where many U.S. companies subcontract their labor; ours is, after all, a free market economy. Popular brands of shoes, like Nike, are produced in Southeast Asia. Levi Strauss once produced all of its jeans in the U.S., and now their factories are in Mexico and Asia. Free market. We can buy Hewlett Packard products made in Mexico and shirts made in Bangladesh. We can purchase almost anything from 25 different countries, but heaven help the senior citizens who dare to buy their prescription drugs from a Canadian or a Mexican Pharmacy.

Buying from outside the country is described by some as "Un-American." Politicians want Americans to obey the law and stop buying illegal drugs. Do you think for a minute that the pharmaceutical companies don't have a powerful lobby? I am hopeful that some federal administration will take a stand. If you have paid for medicine in the last 20 years, then you know that the markup on some medicines is 500% or more. There can be no reason for that other than pure greed.

The important thing to keep in mind is to know and understand what medications your loved one needs, what the adverse reactions might be, and what their schedule is for taking them. There are handy charts that facilitate keeping track of multiple medications available from your local Office on Aging or pharmacy.

In Chapter Eight: Visiting the Hospital, I will give an example of how knowing exactly what Mom was taking benefited her and why. Also, I will discuss why all caregivers should know about possible negative effects of medication.

In addition to the issues of Mom's diet and medications, other concerns included incontinence, bathing, and night restraints.

INCONTINENCE

Over 14 million adults in the U.S. have urinary incontinence. Women over 50 seem to be at the greatest risk, largely as a result of childbirth, aging, and changes in the body. Discussing incontinence is not the most pleasant conversation but is an absolutely necessary one. Incontinence is the actual loss of bladder or bowel control. It brings about that sudden loss of dignity that marks a profound change for an adult, when they are forced to consider using adult diapers. Talk about a behavior shift and a sudden loss of independence! For Mom, I was able to put a portable toilet next to her bed to enable her to keep incontinence at bay during the night.

There are many causes of urinary incontinence. Sometimes it is brought on temporarily by a urinary tract infection and when the infection is cured, the incontinence goes away. It can also be caused by the displacement of the uterus or vagina from pregnancy or weight gain. Age is another factor, usually due to the declining functionality of the nervous system. Certain medications can also be responsible for frequent urination. Other factors that cause urinary leakage include:

- A weak bladder or weakening of the muscles around the bladder
- Damage to the nerves that control the bladder
- A blocked urinary passageway
- Arthritis, which limits movement and can prolong the time it takes to reach the toilet

In men, incontinence can be one of many symptoms of prostate cancer. Separate from the behavioral issues, a major problem related to prostate cancer is denial. Many men are extremely uncomfortable at the mere mention of having a prostate exam, but since it is one of the precautions we can take to control cancer, the test should be encouraged.

BATHING

Bathing can present a difficult challenge, and it did for my mother and me. The very first time I bathed my mother, we went through a metamorphosis, as if we evolved from mother and child, to mother being the child. It was also discomforting since we are not of the same sex. The level of discomfort was apparent from Mom's body language, but we both knew we had to work through it. Eventually, however, Mom was bathed and dressed, and we were able to sit down to breakfast together. I was as happy as she was when we found a female caregiver to take over the bathing duties. But on the weekends, it was just her and me once again. We found our rhythm and discovered that mornings were the best time of day for both of us to get the routine started.

Initial resistance with bathing is another opportunity for you, as caregiver, to remember the word of Dr. Taylor: "Patience."

NIGHT RESTRAINTS

The first night I brought Mom home and put her to bed, she immediately got out and walked to the bathroom without my help. Of course, I was concerned about her falling. The next morning, we had a long conversation about her getting in and out of bed unassisted, but I sensed she wouldn't listen to my reasoning. In fact, a few hours later, I heard her getting up again.

Once more we had the talk, to no avail. Finally, I took a sheet and tied it around her waist to keep her in the bed until I was able to come and assist her. No matter how you look at it or rationalize it, a restraint is horrible. However, I know that for many, restraints provide the protection that is needed.

What do you think my Mom's reaction was to me wrapping the sheet around her? Mom looked at me and said, "Not you! I never thought it would be you." My mother's secret weapon: guilt. She was right all along. Restraints may not have been the right thing to do but was the practical adjustment we needed to make. I was forced to come up with a viable solution on the fly. Mom's thoughts seemed to be going back to where she was the day before. My thoughts were, "What the hell have I gotten myself into?" I made a pallet of some blankets and a pillow beside her bed. When Mom got up in the middle of the night, I was there. I slept with one eye open the whole night.

What do you do when you know the risk of the patient getting up on their own will be a potential disaster? Is the answer about having enough help? Could you have enough nurses and attendants to watch over all of the patients who are at risk of falling? And would that be cost effective? I asked these questions of myself after each visit with Mom. My personal experience with my own mother was an eye-opener. I have researched and asked several people what they think of restraints. It appears to be a subject that is avoided.

You can go to any one of the care facilities in Los Angeles, and you will see patients strapped to their wheelchairs or beds. I saw my Aunt Eva restrained on a visit, asleep in a wheelchair in the hallway of the center. Across her chest was her name, Eva Collier, written with a black marker. Not particularly sophisticated or appealing. The label made it easy for the staff to identify her but left a bad impression for a visitor. I know that Aunt Eva is blind and getting up out of her wheelchair without assistance would be disastrous. She is, after all, 100 years old. I asked about Aunt Eva being restrained and was told that it was for her protection. My view is that we should have a better method of protecting patients from falls and injuries in the 21st Century.

In our homes, however, when safety is an issue, restraints of some kind may be in the best interests of our loved ones. Discuss the issue with their doctor and make the loving choice that will give you all peace of mind.

TRAVEL

Caregiving brings about matters that may not seem obvious at first, such as travel, emergency preparedness, and doctor's visits. But, believe me, caring for Mom shed a light on these subjects.

Traveling can be disconcerting for the senior because of unfamiliar territory, or just the idea of packing and getting ready. If we were scheduled to leave at 8:00 a.m., I would tell Mom that we were leaving at 6:00 a.m. just so we would have a time cushion, and she would not need to rush. We would pack whatever we could a day ahead of time.

My sister Stephanie was instrumental in helping Mom travel. Once, we all went to New York to see my uncle, Illinois Jacquet, play at a benefit concert given in his honor with the world-renowned pianist Dorothy Donegan and the great saxophonist, Grover Washington, Jr.

We were lounging backstage with the musicians and Mom was reveling in it all.

The family and I were all there to help with anything that she needed. At one point during the trip we were moving hurriedly through Penn Station to catch a train and keeping up with us proved difficult for Mom. So my nephew, a college football offensive lineman at the time, literally carried Mom up two flights of stairs, because the nearest elevators were not convenient and time was of the essence. It was quite a memorable scene!

EMERGENCY KITS

Mom was thriving under my care, but as a precaution I developed "the Red Bag"—A red backpack kept next to Mom's bed for emergencies. It contained her vital information and was used whenever Mom had an urgent medical situation and had to be admitted to the hospital. Included in the bag were her medical records, insurance cards, phone numbers of relatives and friends to be called (day or night), doctor's information, Mom's rosary, her Bible, eyeglasses, nightgown, slippers, flashlight, and medications (including over-the-counter medications).

When you visit the doctor with your loved one, you can ask the doctor to note all treatments and medications, together with the dosage and frequency. Otherwise, they might be given drugs that are dangerous in combination with those already being taken, or they might receive too little or too much of their current medications.

Remember to include basic toiletries in the backpack, such as a toothbrush or denture cleaner, deodorant, and razors (for men), because buying them at the hospital is expensive. Pack a few photos that you can display in the hospital room. Also include a tape recorder or notepad for yourself. You don't want to forget what the doctors tell you about tests results, diagnoses, and care instructions for your loved one once they are discharged from the hospital. Don't forget to also pack a few things for yourself, the caregiver.

Waiting is an essential part of the process (see Chapter Eight: Visiting the Hospital). You will want and need something to occupy your time and keep you sustained. For myself, I kept a book, some energy bars, and water in the backpack. Today, I might have added an iPod or other music player to that list, and of course, a cell phone pre-programmed with important contact information.

21ST CENTURY TELEHEALTHCARE

These days, the development and growth of new technologies has made it easier for older patients to remain at home rather than undergo regular doctor visits. Through the use of broadband internet—known as "telehealth"—one nurse or physician can monitor several patients' vital signs remotely and quickly be alerted of any problems. It's the new generation of healthcare. TeleHealthcare.com provides a convenient, affordable solution for your immediate healthcare treatment, and allows immediate access to board-certified, licensed physicians or healthcare professionals in the privacy of your own home. You can choose from a wide range of fields. The costs for services are minimal—all done with online chat or video conferencing—and the services include recommended treatment and prescriptions when appropriate.

IN SUMMARY

Preparing the living environment for your loved one will be challenging, energizing, inspiring, and galvanizing as you utilize the available resources. Be patient and create a plan to be the full-time caregiver. Remind yourself that patience is key to helping your loved one adapt to new surroundings.

WISE TIPS

Medicare will help you pay to set up the house with an adjustable bed, hand rails for hallways and bathrooms, and a safety toilet— if you have private insurance and Medicare, the two will work together to pay some of the home preparation costs.

CAREGIVING QUOTES

As a caregiver in Israel, I have observed many patients who need to be restrained, especially when they are going wild. I have seen social workers here who are patient and some who are not. If an old person is in the hospital and cannot feed themselves or says they don't like to eat, then the workers will not force them. They will just leave. It is so hard to watch that happen to people, because they are old and helpless. When I had a patient like that, I worked with her for 24 hours and tried to give her good care.

— LINDA QUEVADA, 53, Tel Aviv, Israel

In my country, you can do everything with money. Here, we have apartments for old people who have a lot of money, and they get good care and rest. They have doctors, a nurse, and people who look after them. Those who have no money must ask for help from family or other people around them, and it is so sad. But I think that everywhere is the same—when you are old and you have no money, you become trouble for your country, for your family, and for yourself. Only the big love and nice hearts of your family can help you spend the rest of your life like a human being. So many old people have nothing to eat.

— SNEZANA SKOKNA, 47, Belgrade, Serbia

*"It's what you learn after you
know it all that counts."*
— JOHN WOODEN —

CHAPTER 3
Regulating Diet and Exercise

"The sage accumulates nothing, but the more he does for others the greater his existence; the more he gives to others, the greater his abundance."

— LAO TZU

IF YOU WANT your loved ones to avoid diseases and ailments that plague most people as they age, then you must consider what they put into their body. The same holds true for you. What will the thing you consume do once it is inside you? What does a cigarette do to you? How about that nice piece of fried chicken; will it enhance your digestive system or clog it?

Our poor eating habits are often so deeply ingrained that we don't seem to recognize the dangers in poisons like processed fats and dairy products; of "whites" such as bleached flour, pasta, and rice; of stimulants like sugar, caffeine, and nicotine; or of addictive substances like alcohol and illicit drugs. While it is difficult to change our own habits, it may be even more difficult to change those of our loved ones. But if you want to live long and stay out of hospitals, as well as ensure that your loved ones remain as healthy as possible while in your care, proper diet and exercise must become a part of your caregiving routine. Beware of the harm that can result from what you or your loved one consume.

MEAT

Meat, as a rule, is not good for you. Even chicken can be harmful. Former USDA microbiologist Gerald Kuester once stated, "With the advent of modern slaughter technologies, there are about 50 points during processing where cross-contamination can occur. At the end of the line, the birds are no cleaner than if they had been dipped in a toilet."

For some, not eating meat is not an option. If you do eat meat, have it only once a day, and eat it with large portions of water-rich foods. Make sure you have a large salad or steamed vegetables— foods that will cleanse, not clog. Make sure the meal is in the middle of the day. This timing will give your body a chance to digest the meal and more time to put cleansing food into your system. Choose meat that is organic, free-range, and antibiotic-free. Stay away from red meat or have it only once a week. Seafood is a great choice for protein, contains essential fatty acids, and is more nutritious. Make sure the fish is fresh.

Many women believe that they need protein and can only get it from meat—that is a myth. The USDA acknowledges that protein needs can easily be met by eating a variety of plant-based foods. Many world class athletes are vegetarians, including Martina Navratilova, the former great tennis champion; weightlifter, Bill Pearl; Heisman Trophy winner, Desmond Howard; and seven-time Ironman winner, Dave Scott. Protein should make up 5% to 8% of your daily food intake.

SUGAR

Refined sugar should be avoided. Refined sugar is an addictive drug that can contribute to developing diabetes, obesity, coronary thrombosis, tooth decay, gum disease, varicose veins, and stomach problems. Soft drinks contain more sugar than anything else known to humankind. More than 50 million cola beverages are consumed daily in the United States. According to the National Soft Drink Association, the average 12-ounce carbonated soft drink contains the equivalent of 10 teaspoons of sugar and 150 calories. That amount of sugar can immobilize the immune system by about 33%, and about 30 teaspoons can shut it down for an entire day. Artificial sweetness can be just as harmful, with the exception of stevia. There are also healthful substitutes such as pure honey or maple syrup.

CAFFEINE

Coffee in large amounts can be harmful to you. Too much caffeine can affect the cardiovascular system (high blood pressure, high cholesterol levels, arrhythmias or palpitations in the heart), the digestive system (stomach upset, ulcers, diarrhea, reduced nutrient absorption), and energy expenditure. Links have been established between caffeine and bladder cancer in men, and breast cancer in women. And yet, coffee is the world's second most valuable commodity (behind petroleum) in terms of dollars traded. More than 400 billion cups of coffee are consumed every year worldwide. Starbucks did over $2.3 billion in coffee sales according to their 2008 annual report in the first quarter.

ALCOHOL

We are programmed and conditioned to believe that the stimulation from alcohol is good. Turn on any sports program and observe all of the advertising telling you that it is next to impossible to have a good time without a cooler full of ice-cold beer at your disposal. According to Dr. Melvin H. Kinsley of the Medical College of South Carolina in Charleston, "Every time a person takes one drink of alcohol—even a social one—he permanently damages his brain, killing off thousands of brain cells."

TOBACCO

If you are a smoker, then you should know the risks. The U.S. Surgeon General requires the risks to be listed on every type of cigarette packaging and advertisement. Among them are increased risk of heart disease, lung cancer, stroke, emphysema, and hypertension. The American Cancer Society estimated that in 2008, more than 220,000 deaths would be caused by tobacco use alone. So, when you're going to the hospital for your chemo treatments, you can't say that nobody warned you.

SOLUTIONS FOR A HEALTHIER LIFE

- Reduce or eliminate alcohol and tobacco.
- Eat to cleanse.
- Reduce and eliminate acid buildup by consuming a diet consisting of live alkaline foods: dark green and yellow vegetables, soy beans, sprouted nuts, seeds, grains, and essential fatty acids.
- Aim for unprocessed fats in their natural state, such as avocado, almonds, hazelnuts, pumpkin and sunflower seeds, flax seed oil, olive oil, and fish oil.
- Drink water before and after your meals and not during.
- Eat the right food combinations: eat fruit on an empty stomach; eat green vegetables or salad with proteins or with carbohydrates; do not combine fats with proteins.

- Eat in a relaxed state.
- Create your ideal food pyramid: 70% of your diet should be live foods, 10% plant-based proteins or quality fish, 10% carbohydrates, and 10% quality oils.
- Eat organic.

There are also some things that you should never eat again. The reason diets don't work is because you give up soda, fried foods, salt, and sugar for a time—but as soon as you lose the weight, you go back to your old eating habits, and the weight returns. Don't just go on a diet. Change your diet for life.

ILLINOIS JACQUET'S STORY

My mother's baby brother was the great jazz saxophonist, Jean Baptiste Illinois Jacquet. He played music from the time he could walk until his death in 2005, at the age of 82. Uncle Illinois died on a Tuesday and had just performed at the New York Philharmonic the Friday before. Many people at his age are wiping the drool from their mouths. Instead, the only things I remember Uncle licking were the reeds for his saxophone. Watching him prepare to play his instrument was like watching the making of something masterful; like looking over the shoulders of Picasso as he prepared to paint his latest piece of art. The preparation itself is the art form. This fact is illustrated in the opening sequence of "The Texas Tenor," a documentary film about the life of my Uncle Illinois. Leonard Feather, the late jazz critic, hailed Illinois as "one of the five greatest saxophonists in jazz history."

When Uncle Illinois was in his early sixties he decided to change the way he lived his life. He started eating healthily and stopped drinking alcohol. His health improved so dramatically that he played better in his seventies than he did in his sixties. His manager, Carol Scherick, was largely responsible. Carol lived with him for over two decades and made sure that what he put into his body was good for him. She is a vegetarian herself and aware of the benefits of eating right. She made Uncle Illinois her mission.

In 1987 I stopped in to see Uncle Illinois to get his advice on a project. I had just received word that Sony Corporation was going to underwrite the dinner honoring Michael Jackson in New York. It was the first time in the United Negro College Fund history that the dinner had ever been underwritten. Who better to go to for advice than Uncle Illinois? The UNCF headquarters was located in New York and he lived in Queens. It was always a nice ride out to his "crib," and I loved seeing him in a great mood. He spoke with a command that you would expect from a world-famous musician. His advice: "Watch out; someone will try and steal your thunder." But of all the things I remember from that visit, what sticks out is Carol bringing me some freshly squeezed carrot juice. Not that I was expecting a beer or anything, but I knew right away that the brother would have some years ahead of him.

Carol would bring Uncle Illinois' food along with them on the road—food she had prepared herself. She always talked about pesticides and the other dangers of the food we eat. She would even bring his food with them when they would visit Los Angeles and stay at my sister Stephanie's house, traveling with containers of brown rice, bottles of organic fruit and vegetable juices, and no meat in sight.

As Uncle Illinois' manager, Carol brought something very unique to the table. She brought a new way of thinking and taking care of your body, a completely different mindset than the ones typically found around musicians and other entertainers. Carol transformed him into a vegan. There were a lot of obstacles in changing the eating habits of a man who had been doing it his way for so long; a man who would perform a set in a club where drinking alcohol during and after the set was common practice. But at 72, Illinois was so full of energy that he had Bill Cosby jumping up on stage at the Playboy Jazz Festival at the Hollywood Bowl.

IN SUMMARY

This to seniors: Stay active. There are several programs for seniors that include dancing, walking, bowling, and weekend bike rides. Yoga and pool aerobics are great too. It's all important in maintaining a healthy lifestyle. Most food programs target low-income seniors; they are available to all older people regardless of income at many locations.

WISE TIP

When you shop for groceries, read the nutritional value on packages. Most frozen dinners are packed with sodium. The nutritional value of frozen foods varies greatly. Fresh vegetables and fruit will make all the difference. In addition, they are cost-effective.

"Let us remember, so far as we can,
that every unpleasant thought
is a bad thing literally put in the body.
— PRENTICE MULFORD —

CHAPTER 4
Reaching Out to Others

"Helping others represents real power on behalf of God.
— WILSON SIMMONS III

FROM MY PERSONAL experience of caring for my mother, I learned that managing the welfare of our loved ones takes planning, planning, and more planning. I also discovered that family members, friends, church, and other groups can assist with making the transition to becoming a more productive caregiver. Most of the time, however, you have to know whom to ask as well as how to ask. You may fear imposing on others and so, to genuine offers of help you respond, "I can manage; thank you for the offer." The truth is we all need help, and caregivers need more help than most. Yet we don't often ask for it. Asking for help is not easy and knowing how to ask can be a challenge.

I recall a time in Vietnam when I was frustrated with the sergeant-in-charge. Angry and defeated, I wrote to my fiancée, Cecelia Jean, and shared my thoughts. Her return letter provided a simple response: "Wilson, you are a smart man, use your head. Think about how you can turn that situation around to your benefit." I did, and it changed my reality. I went from feeling total anger and frustration to being in control of my own destiny, because I changed my mindset. Cecellia's words still resonate with me today, and they serve as an anchor for how one can change their state of being in any situation through changing their approach. I changed my approach to providing care for Mom by including others, and the benefits were amazing

As the weeks of caregiving went by, I would call my sisters in Los Angeles and ask, "Can you give me a weekend this month or next when you can take care of Mom?" It worked beautifully. I had been quick to apologize for my behavior when we had disagreed about how to approach Mom's caregiving. I was sorry and making amends made my life a lot easier.

Most importantly, I learned that not everyone is a caregiver. It was not effective for me to point fingers at family members who didn't participate in Mom's care. Over time, other family members did enough finger-pointing for me, realizing one day they might be in the very same shoes as those now needing care. My advice: learn from the process; don't blame. Love truly conquers all. I provide some other ways to approach family members for assistance later in this chapter.

The telephone was my favorite tool to use for asking friends and family if they would help me. I also used a planner to keep myself on schedule, a strategy I had learned while working as the National Marketing Manager for the United Negro College Fund, making over 200 calls a day from my office. I would create a daily to-do list of ten things I wanted to accomplish and would follow through until everything was done.

While caring for Mom, I used the same strategy to recruit assistance. I generally made 30 to 50 or so calls every morning, to family members, churches, organizations, doctors, nurses, and my own social network, from 9:00 a.m. to 10:30 a.m., which was the time it took for the home-care aide to bathe Mom and dress her. As soon as the aide arrived, I would be on the phone. The contact numbers were already in order for me to call, along with the day's objective. On most days, I would talk to roughly 15 or 20 people. Most of the time I made follow-up calls in the afternoon. If using the phone is not your thing, find a family member who can make calls. Making calls takes skill and, again, patience.

One of the jewels in taking care of my mother was the great Dr. Mary Taylor, who had been Mom's primary care physician. She was not only qualified, she was a Black doctor, and that thrilled Mom to no end. Her office was near Brotman Hospital in Culver City, and Mom saw her twice a month. Dr. Taylor always answered all of my questions, and I always had a ton of them. I wanted to know the purpose of each medication prescribed for Mom, and what the possible side effects were.

More than a few doctors raised their eyebrows when I asked questions. The most interesting were the doctors who were condescending. The life of your loved one is at stake, but you shouldn't ask questions? My questioning may have bruised some egos and hurt some feelings, but I wanted answers. Before the explosion of the Internet, I practically lived in the library. Downtown Los Angeles has one of the greatest libraries in the country. Even with the instant nature of the Internet, the library is still a wonderful and always reliable source of information.

Sometimes the calls that I needed to make were to friends or family members, and they would want to chat a little longer than anticipated. Since I had lists of things I wanted done, I would say, "I was about to call Brian to see if he can water the plants once a week, maybe you could do that?" Suddenly, I would be able to end the conversation. If someone said they would bring Mom a magazine or book and I didn't hear from them, I would call and add something to their list. Eventually, they would get the message and became pretty prompt in responding. It is the small gestures that make a difference.

Before long, the house was always full of activity. On a typical Friday, Mom would have the regular aide, someone watering the plants, a physical therapist, and a couple of visitors. It was a coordinated effort.

Help can be closer than you think. Many of the tools you need may be right at your fingertips. Think of the people you know who may have resources or connections to get things that your loved one needs or enjoys. Think about what would make your loved one's life easier, as well as your own life as a caregiver. Compile a list of what makes your loved one happy or what they enjoyed doing when they were independent but can no longer do. Then find a way to make those things happen.

Mom had a built-in network that was virtually untapped. Besides the obvious family members and association of extended family, you can almost always rely on the church. Most churches have a person whose job it is to visit the members who have become shut-ins, including sick people in hospitals or care facilities. To get their help however, you must ask. Otherwise, they won't know. When Mom was too weak to go to Mass, I requested a priest to come and give her communion.

Since Mom was one of the first teachers in the Los Angeles- area Head Start program, I tapped into that network of former colleagues and students. Mom was also a long-standing member of the Knights of Peter Claver Ladies Auxiliary, a Catholic organization. It is part of the duty of members to visit and pray for the sick. They also attend funerals. I once joked with Mom when she was in her sixties because she was always attending funerals in her white outfit. I would say, "Mom, at this rate, since most of the members are seniors, when do you have time to do anything else?" She looked me straight in the eye and wagged her finger at me and laughed. Now I could recruit these women to come and visit my mom.

My brothers from the Omega Psi Phi fraternity played a big role in assisting me with a number of recommendations and resources, including obtaining food as well as a brand-new refrigerator and stove. A lot of the old Qs, as Omegas are often called, just stopped by and brought flowers and cards. The gesture was awesome! Mom knew most of my frat brothers from my days in college. Their visits often gave me energy when I needed it most. Our unofficial sister sorority, Delta Sigma Theta, was quite helpful as well with information and the Delta's Senior Center.

Support can even be found from neighbors (old and new), clients (present or former), political organizations, business associates, volunteer groups, community centers, senior centers, student nurses, and old classmates.

The most important thing to remember about asking for support, however, is to be specific in your requests. "Yes, I can use help" really doesn't give a clear picture of what you need. Here are some of the ways I solicited aid, both personal and professional:

- **Find a terrific caregiver**. One of my sisters worked in King Drew Medical Hospital for many years and was able to provide an excellent recommendation for someone to be Mom's first caregiver.
- **Find a nurse's aide**. Someone in your church or community might be able to make a recommendation. You might also place an ad in the paper. Service agencies, such as Medicaid, will also provide aides, but they are not necessarily the most qualified. Interviews are necessary for anyone you invite to care for your loved one.

- **Read stories or poems aloud to your loved one**. My mother loved poetry, and we were fortunate to have many family members who loved to come by to read. Reading not only shares a good story, it provides company as well.
- **Take your loved one for a drive**. A couple of friends and family members enjoyed this almost as much as Mom! Family members would share in taking Mom to have her nails done. Jon, another dear friend, would take Mom to Catholic Mass and then drive out to the Santa Monica Pier to look at the ocean.
- **Help with the shower or bath**. On the weekends, it was helpful to have a family member lend a hand to bathe Mom. One of my sisters enjoyed the time it took to bathe Mom. Her soothing tone of assurance was a gift.
- **Bring magazines or a book for your loved one to enjoy**. People brought Mom so many magazines to read that I was relieved to be able to stop buying them.
- **Bring music**. Mom loved Nina Simone, Ella Fitzgerald and Billie Holiday. The caregiver might appreciate the music as well!
- **Change the linens**. This is often done by the caregiver, who will welcome the break. Maggie was my backup, and also did a wonderful job of washing clothes when needed.
- **Give your loved one a massage**. In my opinion, this is one of the best gifts you can give. I had a friend who was a professional masseuse and she gave Mom a discounted rate. It was worth the price just to hear Mom purr.
- **Water the plants**. That was my "angel" Eboni's thing. She did it every time she was in town.
- **Take your loved one to a Senior Center for a few hours**. Some centers even provide pick-up and drop-off services. In Los Angeles, it is the Delta Sigma Theta Center. Check for one in your city.
- **Make a collage of family photos**. This may also help stimulate and retain your loved one's memory, as well as help them remember better days. Maggie and Auntie Laura did a wonderful job of gathering pictures and creating an awesome collage for Mom to enjoy.

- **Wash your loved one's hair or take them to have it professionally styled**. Taking Mom out "to get her hair done" was a favorite of Eboni's. Mom was always full of energy after having her hair done. Like most of us, looking good made her feel good.
- **Treat your loved one to a manicure and pedicure**. For Mom, a "mani-pedi" ranked up there with having her hair done. Virginia was the go-to person for that, and she found a place right near Mom's house that did an excellent job.
- **Cook a meal, or go out to eat**. Whenever Mom was away from home, she took advantage of not having to abide by the healthy diet that I was feeding her, and she indulged in her favorites, like gumbo and jambalaya. She didn't think I knew. Pat knew the spots.
- **Take out the garbage**. Anyone who stopped by would see a list of things-to-do posted on the wall. A gesture as small as taking out the trash was always appreciated.
- **Offer to relieve the primary caregiver for a weekend (or longer)**. Although infrequent, this was a very big help to me, and a nice change of scenery for Mom. Stephanie and Maggie both stepped up big-time with that.
- **Offer to pick up the prescription refills from the pharmacy**. This is a big time-saver for the person who normally does it, and Aunt Eva was the go-to person.
- **Handle your loved one's finances, or find someone whom you trust to do it**. Taking care of Mom's finances was my job.
- **Write letters on behalf of your loved one (let them dictate to you)**. Mom had a network of friends to whom she would want cards and other correspondence mailed. It became a group effort to get everything written and sent. Today we have the Internet; emails will do the same thing.
- **Watch your loved one's favorite TV shows with them**. Mom watched "The Young and the Restless" religiously. When I took some time to watch it with her, I still didn't get the fascination, but at least had some idea what she was talking about when she would talk to the TV, and later to Stephanie and Yvette Coleman, about what Victor Newman was up to.

- **Be a problem solver**. I took ownership for that, because problems are the order of the day for a caregiver. Everyone has a complaint or knows a better way of doing things, only they don't want to do it themselves. It is the proverbial critic who is quick to point out what should and could be done. From that end, I agree with President Theodore Roosevelt, "...it is not the critic who counts, it's the man in the arena whose face is marred by blood and sweat.."

IN SUMMARY

Utilize the network of friends, churches, colleagues, and organizations to assist you along the way. There is an untapped network of resources. The 21st Century has spawned the Social Network, which is not a fad but now the way to communicate needs, ideas, and assistance. Caregivers require support, recognition, and respite. It is necessary to maintain your own physical, emotional, and social well-being. Most of the help is just a click away on your computer. Don't have one? Your local library has several.

WISE TIP

In a study by Care Net, it was found that more than 50% of the caregivers turned first to other family members for assistance yet, sadly, nearly 66% reported receiving no help or very little help from them. Only 16% said they sought help most often from public or private agencies.

CHAPTER 5
Preparing for Difficult Behavior

"If there is no struggle, there is no progress."
— FREDERICK DOUGLAS

CAREGIVING IS A test of perseverance, stamina, and dedication. The caregiver becomes responsible for another's well-being, while trying to maintain their own. Of course, not everyone's situation with caretaking will be the same but it is always wise to be prepared for whatever may occur. With Mom, some difficult behavior patterns cropped up, bringing on a whole new set of challenges for me.

Following are some of the typical behaviors that may occur while you are caring for a loved one. In order to cope with the behaviors, first understand the nature of the behavior problem. Is the behavior harmful to your loved one, yourself, or others? Second, what may have happened before that led to the behavior? Keep a journal of the time and place a behavior begins. You will be able to identify triggers that possibly contribute to the difficulties.

WANDERING

One day, before I started taking care of my mother full-time, Stephanie and I took Mom to the movie theater. While we were enjoying the movie, Mom excused herself and said she was going to the restroom. After a few minutes, I asked Stephanie to go check on her. My sister came back in a hurry and said that Mom was not in the restroom. I got up, and we looked around the theater, but Mom was nowhere to be found. We left the theater to look for her outside and found her standing next to Stephanie's car.

"Mom!" We screamed at once, "What are you doing out here?" Mom looked at us as if we were both space cadets and said, "I have been waiting on you two. What took you so long?"

This was a new experience for us all. Mom was still living on her own at the time, but this innocent family outing had ignited our search for a part-time caregiver. We began to insist that Mom carry identification with her at all times. Stephanie bought a nice leather pouch for Mom to wear around her waist to hold her I.D. and other needed items. Mom continued to love going to the movies but was never allowed to go to the restroom alone again.

ANGER/AGITATION

Sometimes your loved one's agitation has to do with something as simple as being thirsty or hungry. At other times, it is with their knowing they are not going to get better whether from declining health or an incurable disease from which they are suffering. When you have done just about everything that you can do and have explored all avenues with no ultimate solution, anger generally manifests. If those emotions are held inside, they often lead to depression. No one wants to be sick or old. No one wants to become a burden to others.

It is a fact that listening solves or eases a lot of these problems. Let your loved ones express how they are feeling, without interruption. Give them an outlet to let it all go. Ask what's wrong. Be compassionate about how they are feeling. You may have done everything right but find it difficult to understand what all the fuss is about. Allow them to vent, and even encourage it. Get a pad and write the problem down. Discuss the behavior with their doctor. Consult their peer group and your assisting friends and relatives to see how others in similar situations deal with their emotions. There is also an infinite number of support groups online as well as numerous forums to explore. Use them.

ISOLATION AND LONELINESS

The fear of isolation—physical, social, and emotional—can result from chronic illness. Physically-confined patients lose the opportunity to socialize with friends and often find themselves withdrawing further from them. The fear of isolation usually doesn't occur immediately after a diagnosis. It takes time for ill patients or stay-at-home seniors to pull away from society or to recognize that friends, family acquaintances, and co-workers may be avoiding them. Without dedicated caregivers, friends, and relatives that care enough to show up and be present during an illness or confinement, the patient can, over time, become a hermit or shut-in, not seeing many people for a long time. Sometimes only one son or daughter or caregiver is left to shoulder the entire burden.

PARANOIA

Paranoia is somewhat common among seniors. They will tell you that someone has taken something from their bedroom. It is easy for seniors to misplace things, and when they can't find something, they often blame it on the caregiver, aide, maid, or another family member.

I would have to constantly reassure my mother that no one wanted her coat (the one she almost never wore but was convinced had been stolen). It didn't matter what I said. Generally, I would just listen and tell her that I would get to the bottom of it. Once, when her favorite scarf was "missing" and I could not find it, she perked up and said, "See? I told you so. That woman stole my red scarf!"

When eventually I found the scarf under a bundle of just-laundered clothes, I put it around Mother's neck. She stood in front of the mirror and gazed at her reflection for a minute, then she laughed so hard that she "peed." Incontinence. Life is full of surprises.

Medication is sometimes responsible for the paranoia. Check with the doctor and discuss whether this problem could be a side effect of a particular drug or interaction of two or more.

DEPRESSION

Depression is one of the greatest problems and killers of our time, and it will be the second largest killer, after heart disease, very soon. Today, nearly 20 million adults of the U.S. population suffer from depression. And yet, according to the National Healthcare Quality Report, published in 2004, 80% of depressed people are not currently having any treatment.

Caring for a depressed loved one can be a burden. Too often the caregiver will feel trapped or imprisoned in their own household. More than 30% of women are depressed, and they make up the majority of those giving care. The National Mental Health Association estimated that 43% of depressed women are too embarrassed to seek help. The truth is that, most adults are never treated. If you have been independent all of your life, and now someone has taken your car keys and is making decisions you have made all of your life, that is reason enough to be depressed. Most people believe that depression is a personal weakness. Acknowledge your loved one's depression, as well as your own. You can do something about it.

Symptoms of Depression to watch for:
- Restlessness and irritability
- Sleep disturbances, lack of energy, tiredness
- Excessive crying
- Loss of interest or pleasure in everyday activities
- Oversleeping, insomnia, waking up earlier
- Persistent sadness, anxiety, or empty moods
- Difficulty remembering, focusing, or making small decisions
- Feelings of helplessness, guilt, worthlessness, or hopelessness
- Thoughts of suicide or death, or suicide attempts
- Loss of memory, concentration, or decision-making capability
- Change in appetite or weight
- Loss of interest in sex
- Aches and pains that don't go away when treated
- Poor self-image or self esteem

Diagnosis and Treatment

The first step to taking charge of your observation is to visit a doctor, preferably a mental health specialist, for diagnosis and treatment. Diagnosis is often difficult to make, because clinical depression can manifest in so many different ways. For instance, some clinically-depressed individuals seem to withdraw into a state of apathy. Others may become irritable or even agitated, and their eating and sleeping patterns can be exaggerated.

Most depressed people who seek treatment can feel better within a very short period of time, but different therapies seem to work for different people. For example, support groups can provide new coping skills or social support when you are dealing with a major life change. Also, don't forget to call on family and friends to help provide support.

Ask the doctor about medications, such as antidepressants, and other options that can help. Some medications will help improve sleep, appetite, and concentration.

COMMUNICATION

As Mom suffered more strokes, communication became more difficult. I was forced to simplify information to assist her in understanding things. I thought it would be a good idea if Mom and I could type each other letters on a computer, even though she was still speaking pretty well. We would be communicating at a new level. Since Mom had typed more than a hundred words a minute when she worked, I thought maybe her fingers would do what her mouth couldn't.

We talked about using the computer, and she was all set to type, but when she tried, it just didn't work. She no longer had the touch. The after-effects of her strokes had made pressing the keys and forming simple words nearly impossible. Mom would touch a key and ten of the same character would appear on the screen. She tried really hard. I cried just watching her. We were getting down to just plain, short, simple sentences, giving one direction at a time. "Mom, it's time to eat." "Mom, I love you very much." Toward the end of our sessions, I could tell from her eyes what she wanted me to do, as they were clearer than any words—typed or spoken.

INSOMNIA

When it comes to a good night's sleep, do you ever feel like the old and the restless? "If only I could get a good night's sleep" is a common complaint, particularly among older Americans. Many seniors have trouble falling asleep and staying asleep, due to symptoms that can cause daytime fatigue, impair normal functioning and, yes, even cause crankiness. If this describes you, keep reading. Maybe this section will put you to sleep.

Eating and Drinking Before Bed

- Drink some warm milk—even take a warm soothing bath. Women seem to be better at this than men.
- Don't smoke; if you do, it might be a good idea to stop. Nicotine can cause sleeplessness.
- Do not drink coffee or tea, especially in the evening, because caffeine is a stimulant. If you wish to drink tea in the evening, make it decaffeinated.
- Soft drinks are the worst—read the labels.

Before Getting Into Bed

- Do not take naps during the day.
- Exercise—Take a walk, do some light yoga, stretch a little, just enough to relax your muscles and get ready for bed. This can help to ease the tension, and quiet a busy mind. When your body is relaxed, you can sleep so much easier.
- Do not watch television or listen to the radio in the bedroom before going to sleep. I know—that is almost impossible in today's world.
- Avoid eating large meals and snacks before bedtime.
- Avoid alcoholic drinks. Alcohol produces "rebound insomnia," causing you to wake up shortly after falling asleep, with difficulty going to sleep again.

After Getting Into Bed

- The bedroom should be dark and comfortably cool.
- Meditation is an excellent way to eliminate body tension and anxiety. Try to clear your mind of all distractions and relax. Meditating before going to sleep, either through prayer, silence, or being grateful for who you are, what you have, or what has happened to you today, is a good exercise to develop. Counting backwards from 100 does the same thing for many people
- Go to bed at the same time five to seven nights a week.

Treatment for Chronic Insomnia

- Behavioral techniques to improve sleep, such as relaxation therapy and sleep reconditioning. The most commonly used treatment that may help with insomnia is to recondition yourself to associate the bed and bedtime with sleep. For most people, this means not using their beds for any activities other than sleep and sex rather than watching TV or playing on the laptop.
- As part of the reconditioning process, the person is usually advised to go to bed only when sleepy. If unable to fall asleep, the person is told to get up, stay up until sleepy and then return to bed. Throughout this process, the person should avoid naps and wake up and go to bed at the same time each day. Eventually the person's body will be conditioned to associate the bed with bedtime sleep.
- Diagnosing with your doctor to determine medical, psychological or behavioral causes.
- Sleeping pills, although long-term use of sleeping pills for chronic insomnia is not recommended. Consult your doctor.

DEPENDENCY

Encourage independence. If an aging parent or the loved one that you are caring for is no longer able to earn a living, find something that will assist them in feeling useful. Most seniors enjoy the independence of driving. Once that is taken away, you will need to be creative about keeping them active.

If your loved one is capable of cooking, planning weekly menus, making out the grocery list, or paying the bills, give them the job. They will love being a part of the process of daily living. Use whatever available skills there are for as long as you can.

IN SUMMARY

When seniors reach that age where they can no longer take care of themselves, don't expect a personality change. They still will attempt to order you around but remember that they will want to maintain their independence at all costs.

WISE TIPS

Find a support group where your parent or your loved one can share their feelings. If it's your husband and he is physically abusive, you should take measures to keep him from hurting you or himself. It might be time to consider a nursing facility. That goes for your parents or loved ones as well.

CAREGIVING QUOTES

My advice to someone providing caregiving is to try to get support and take some time off for you, for your mental health and well-being. Also, do not take things personally when the person you are caring for says things that might hurt your feelings, because they are not themselves. Just be there to care for them and love them unconditionally. The toughest part of caregiving for me was not getting enough support from my family. I was fortunate to have my sister's help, but we both held fulltime jobs. I worked during the day and my sister worked the nightshift. Even with the two of us, it was still difficult at times, because medica-tion had to be given at specific times.
— KAREN CRAWLEY, Ontario, Canada

Please caution your readers about the tobacco issue. I spent a dozen years as an eldercare assisted living regulator for two counties in Maryland. I did regular announced and unannounced inspections of homes, which included private talks with residents, so I got to know many of them fairly well. Along the way I experienced three instances where doctors and adult children successfully pressured healthy, active, "with it" elders into stopping smoking. In each of those cases, dementia set in within a few months, followed by death within a year. When an individual has been smoking for 50-60 years, nicotine has become a substantial part of their brain chemistry and that of their general bio-systems. To stop naturally impairs cognitive function, and it would be logical to assume it would have an effect on metabolism, energy, and immunities as well. My advice is to tread very carefully regarding the smoking issue.

—Deborah Louis, PhD in Human & Social Development & Behavior

CHAPTER 6
Senior Driving

"Many people don't actually lie; they merely present the truth in such a way that nobody recognizes it."

— ELEANOR HOLMES NORTON

THE PRIVILEGE OF driving is a very touchy topic to address with a loved one, and as a result we often neglect to recognize the early warning signs of driving problems. Drivers aged 65 and older have a higher crash-death rate per driver than all other groups except teenagers. From 1990 to 1997, motor vehicle deaths rose 14% among senior drivers, and non-fatal injuries among the same group rose 19%. Deaths from motor vehicle accidents are twice as likely to be caused by men over the age of 65—the 65-and-older age group is the fastest growing segment of the population. The fact is that more than 40 million seniors were licensed drivers by the year 2020. According to the National Institute on Aging, it is estimated that more than 650,000 people age 70 or older stop driving each year, but it is around the age of 85 that most seniors give up the keys.

Many seniors tend to drive solely in the areas near their home and drive to places which are familiar. It is when they venture out of their comfort zone that their vulnerability is exposed. They may decide to venture off on a night run when they are normally used to driving during the daylight hours. The statistics show that over 80% of accidents involving seniors happen during the night. Glaring lights and less-than-perfect visibility can spell trouble. The same can be said for bad weather, rush hour traffic, or unfamiliar roads. These variables are capable of bringing the average senior to a halt.

The first time I asked my mother to give up the keys to her car, she said, "Get lost!" She didn't hesitate or stutter. She walked off like I wasn't even standing there. I remember thinking, "This is going to be harder than I thought." Mom had recently been involved in an automobile accident. She was not at fault and was going through the usual process with her auto insurance carrier. She went on about her routine without giving me a second thought. I was standing at the front door of her home and she walked right past me on her way out.

It would be another three weeks before we would have the conversation again. She'd had another accident. I stood in the same place in Mom's house and before I could say a word to her, she blurted out, "It wasn't my fault." I didn't say anything. I just hugged Mom and asked her where the keys were. She handed them over. The look on her face was one of resignation.

For safety's sake, take a drive with your loved one (if you dare), and find out for yourself how they stack up. Do they have trouble signaling or navigating a turn? Making a left turn in busy city traffic is a challenge for the seasoned pro—it's chaotic, and people are often still turning after the light has changed to red. It is one of the hazards of the road.

Driving in the wrong lane is also a good indicator and warning sign of confusion. Being able to drive with the flow of traffic is very important. You see it all the time in the city: the speed limit reads 35 miles per hour and the senior is going about 20.

Does your loved one often appear agitated or irritated with the other drivers on the road? When they park the car, do they always hit the curb? How is their peripheral vision? Look around in their garage. Are there scrapes and dents on the car? What about along the inside walls of the garage? You can generally tell if a parent has had a difficult time parking in the garage.

Have you ever seen someone stop in the middle of the street for no apparent reason? This happens routinely. Sometimes the senior driver is looking for an address, but often this is an older driver being overly careful. Does your loved one get lost often? Look for signs of dementia or Alzheimer's disease, and consult with their doctor. When possible, it's helpful if you can take your parents off driving gradually rather than stopping them cold.

TOP 10 REASONS TO TAKE AWAY SENIORS' KEYS

1. Their reaction time is altered, often as a result of illness.

2. They have poor eyesight. Many illnesses can cause vision problems, and diabetes tops the list.
3. Their hearing is impaired.
4. Their decision-making ability may be impaired by dementia or other illness.
5. They are easily confused and/or lost.
6. Their mobility and/or strength have diminished.
7. Their medication may cause drowsiness.
8. They may cause an accident.
9. They are often unable to complete a driver's safety program for seniors.
10. Their doctor gives the order for them to stop driving.

I was a witness to a tragic example of a senior who held onto his keys too long. Some years ago, I shopped every Wednesday at the open-air Farmers Market in Santa Monica that offers fresh fruit and vegetables for sale, much of it organic. In the summer of 2003, an 86-year-old man lost control of his car killing ten people as he barreled for three blocks through the crowded street market. Eight people, including a three- year-old girl, died at the scene of the accident—two others died later at the hospital. Dozens of people were hurt, many critically, including children, among them a 7-month-old boy who suffered major head injuries and other trauma.

Afterwards, I followed the story in the newspaper. Some time prior to the accident, the elderly driver had been asked to give up his keys but refused. He had a history of mishaps and his garage was full of dings and dents. He would not listen to anyone in his family when they expressed concern for his declining driving ability.

The City of Santa Monica charged the man with vehicular manslaughter and brought him to trial. When he appeared in court, he was using a walker, looking old and frail. No doubt his intention was to look as old as he could in order to get sympathy from the court. Some news reporters questioned his sincerity and wrote about the perceived ruse for sympathy. If it were a ruse, it worked. His stubbornness had caused the loss of life and untold suffering, and now he stood before a judge and a jury to see if he would go to prison. The man's sole defense was that he had stepped on the accelerator instead of the brake. The jury found him not guilty, but the City of Santa Monica was held liable for failing to have a barrier preventing vehicles from plowing through the market. The city did install steel barriers later.

WHAT TO DO WHEN IT'S TIME TO TAKE AWAY THE KEYS

If your loved one offers strong resistance, but you know that their driving represents a clear and present danger, drastic measures may be the only alternative. Experts suggest the following strategies:

- Bring all of the family together to discuss what needs to be done.
- Collect and share headlines from stories of seniors involved in fatal traffic accidents.
- Disable your loved one's vehicle if necessary.
- Donate the car to charity. Usually the car can be included as a tax write-off.
- As a last resort, report your loved one to the authorities. The DMV will revoke their license.
- If you don't know what to do, consult with someone who does.
- Of course, someone can simply take the keys.

IN SUMMARY

Most seniors fight for their right to keep driving. For many, it is their last real piece of independence. Driving allows you to come and go when you please. More importantly, a driver does not have to depend on anyone. The right to drive is one of the last big things worth fighting for, and many seniors will tell you flat out that they are not giving up the keys. Period. It has been said that it is easier to give up your spouse than your car.

WISE TIPS

Disabled Department of Motor Vehicle (DMV) Placard—If your loved one gives up the privilege of driving, the placard will be a life saver. You can apply for a Temporary or Permanent Personal Parking Permit by downloading a form from your local motor vehicle facility website. Take the application form to a doctor to fill out the physician's portion. Please note that this permit is only to be used when the patient is a passenger in the car.

CAREGIVING QUOTES
(ON THE SUBJECT OF SENIOR DRIVERS)

Florence is "86 years young" and has been driving her beautiful silver Jaguar to church on Sundays to meet with her girlfriends, to play bridge at the Yacht Club, to go grocery shopping, and to pick up her prescriptions at the local pharmacy. In an interview with her, I asked about her driving, and she told me very simply that she was a good driver. She said, "I had a small accident in the parking lot, but other than that, I am driving well." She said that she would be glad to have someone ride with her and evaluate her driving. In further discussion with her daughter, who is the chief caregiver, I discovered that the "small accident in the parking lot" caused over $10,000 worth of damage to her car. Florence had stepped on the accelerator instead of the brakes and smashed in the hood of the Jaguar. Florence has not given up driving, although most of it is now done within a two-mile radius.

— FLORENCE, 86, Long Beach, California

My Aunt Eva visited Mom two or three times a week while I was taking care of her. She almost always parked two feet from the curb. I would say to her, "Darling, you are parked almost in the middle of the street." She would laugh out loud and throw me her keys, and I would move her car closer to the curb. Aunt Eva drove all over the city until she was 95-years old. I asked her one day what motivated her to cut down the amount of driving she did. She answered, "I could barely see the road, and couldn't see anything at all on the right side." She would drive slowly, and this was in the City of Los Angeles, where they impatiently honk their horns if you don't speed off the moment the light turns green. Aunt Eva would never get on the freeways, and she also avoided left turns in busy intersections. She had a regular routine, and it was limited to going to Mass and visiting her family and friends.

— EVA COLLIER, 100, Los Angeles, California

Mr. King has been driving since he was a kid. He has now reached an age where driving is his last hope of independence. His oldest daughter is his caregiver and she worries about his being in an accident. The idea that he should not be driving is not one he is ready to concede. He is alert, articulate, and quite opinionated. Mr. King grew up in Pittsburgh and was a business owner for many years. He drives to church and to run a few errands, and seldom ventures more than five miles from home. Experiencing some health issues, as is expected at his age, he has four daughters who each have a hand in caring for him. The main caregiver does the bulk of the work, but she is supported by the other daughters. One daughter, Donna, lives in Los Angeles. Another, Aldine, lives in Portland, Oregon, and the youngest daughter lives in New York. Recently, Mr. King suffered a setback in his health and had to be hospitalized. Since his return home, driving has been a non-issue. No one says anything about it, but all of his girls were at his side.

—DOUGLAS KING, 93, Pittsburgh, PA

Did I stop driving voluntarily? No, but I found that it was not a problem for me to stop. I was 40 years old before I learned to drive. However, I did enjoy having my own car so that I could go and come without waiting on someone else. Later in years, I was glad that I could chauffeur my parents when they could no longer drive, and finally ended up transporting both parents and my husband to doctors' appointments, the hospital, etc. I later developed sleep apnea, and after going to sleep at a red light and undergoing many sleep tests, we made the decision for me to stop driving. And believe me, now I enjoy being driven around.

— ELIZABETH WILKS, 86, Chicago, IL

CHAPTER 7
Recognizing Health Issues

"We've got a thousand different diagnoses and diseases out there. They're just the weak link. They're all the result of one thing: stress. If you put enough stress on the chain and you put enough stress on the system, then one of the links breaks."

—DR. BEN JOHNSON

THERE ARE NUMEROUS concerns for the possible health issues that may occur while loved ones are in our care, and their doctors are the best source of information for these concerns. However, the health issues included in this section are intended to help you become informed and aware of some of the possibilities so you might better recognize them if they occur.

TRANSIENT ISCHEMIC ATTACKS (TIAs): THE "MINI-STROKE"

According to the American Stroke Association, more than 600,000 people in America have mini-strokes each year. Known as Transient Ischemic Attacks, or "TIAs," they occur when the blood supply to part of the brain is briefly interrupted. They usually occur suddenly and are very similar to a regular stroke, but they don't last as long. The symptoms sometimes include paralysis, numbness, and dizziness. The major difference between a TIA and a normal stroke is that TIAs go away in less than a day and leave no lasting damage. That is also one of the reasons that they are often ignored. If you believe you have or a loved one has suffered a mini-stroke, check with your doctor. In most cases, a TIA is a precursor to a real stroke in the future. For some it could happen within the next month and for others it may be the next year. Don't speculate. Have it checked out.

Is It a Stroke?

The signs of stroke come in many forms. I mistook my own episode with Bell's Palsy (paralysis of cranial nerve) for a stroke, and if it had been a stroke I would have put myself in jeopardy—perhaps, even died. Why? Foolishly, I had waited until the next morning, after experiencing symptoms, before I went to the hospital. I can't tell you what I was thinking. Obviously, I wasn't thinking. Not clearly anyway.

I had been on the job, working. I had done my usual thing, arriving at the office before anyone else and leaving after everyone was gone. The difference was that at the time, I was a 63-year-old black male with high blood pressure. I worked out every day and ate all the right foods—no salt, no red meat or fried foods. I drank lots of water, ate tons of fruits and vegetables; but still, my age, race, and family history were not in my favor.

One particular night on the job, I was talking with Jenny, the sister from Finance. She was telling me that she had overheard the boss talking about moving me out of the cubicle and putting me in an office. It was around 7 p.m. and everyone else was gone. She was showing me the office and, all of sudden, I felt a kind of jolt from my forehead. I felt my face go numb and excused myself. I headed to my car and started the drive home to Los Angeles.

The office was in South Pasadena and the road back to Los Angeles is a winding highway of about three miles that runs past Dodger Stadium and downtown Los Angeles. All the way home, I was doing a self-check. I tried to whistle but couldn't purse my lips. I couldn't pronounce words that start with "B." I had yet to look at my face in a mirror but could feel the numbness and some discomfort in my left eye. Whenever I blinked, something just didn't feel right. I cursed out loud, "Damn! I've had a stroke."

When I arrived home, I went straight to the bathroom and my worst fears were realized. The side of my face was sagging. "Damn, damn, damn. It's my own damn fault," I muttered to myself. For some reason, I went to the bedroom and did 20 pushups with no problem. Next, I made myself a cup of green tea, as though it were some magical formula. I was sitting on the edge of the bed, getting ready to take the first sip, when it spilled down my chin because I couldn't position my lips to drink it. "Oh crap!" I thought, and instead of going to the hospital right away, I went to sleep.

Early the next morning, I went to the emergency room of the VA hospital. The admitting nurse asked the usual questions— "What's the emergency?" "I've had a stroke," I replied, matter of factly. She asked, "How do you know you had a stroke?" I explained the events that had taken place the night before and pointed to my face. She hurriedly brought me to the examination area and took my blood pressure. And for the next five hours I was treated as a stroke victim. The thoughts that ran through my brain during that time were enough to cause me to pause and consider the path I had taken in life. I was powerless as I lay on the gurney next to all those ailing veterans. I did some more silent cursing to myself, and up until I was diagnosed with Bell's Palsy, I was certain that I'd had a stroke, because the symptoms are so similar.

Strokes are the third leading cause of death in the United States, and the leading cause of serious, long-term disability. About 650,000 new strokes and close to 200,000 resulting deaths are reported in the United States annually. Caring for my mother gave me firsthand knowledge of how stroke can permanently affect one's quality of life.

Warning signs of a stroke include weakness or numbness in the face, which is what I felt with Bell's Palsy. With a stroke, there is also weakness in the arms and or legs, often on one side of the body. The stroke victim may have trouble speaking or understanding others when being spoken to, again, depending on severity. Changes in eyesight, such as dimness, double vision, or a complete loss of vision, as well as dizziness or sudden falls, can also be signs. One might encounter a loss of balance or just plain unsteadiness, a headache, or a sudden sharp pain in the face. The smart thing to do if you experience anything close to these symptoms is to call 911 immediately. Don't be stupid and wait until the next day, like Yours Truly, El Stupido.

The National Stroke Association developed the acronym "F.A.S.T." to help recognize the symptoms of stroke. If you think that you or someone you know is having a stroke, do this simple test:

Face:	Ask the person to smile. Does one side droop?
Arms:	Ask the person to raise both arms. Does one arm drift downward?

| **Speech**: | Ask the person to repeat a simple sentence. Are the words slurred? Can they repeat the sentence correctly? |
| **Time**: | If the person shows any of these symptoms, time is important. Call 911 or get to the hospital fast. Brain cells are dying. |

Here's another simple test: Ask the person to stick out their tongue. If the tongue is crooked or is drooping to one side, that is also an indication of a stroke.

Remember these warning signs, because the life you save may be your own. If you can get a stroke victim to the hospital within three hours of the onset, the effects of the stroke can be totally reversed. Totally. The trick is to recognize the symptoms and get medical care within that 3-hour window—which can be tough to do in today's hospital system.

Ralph's Story

Dr. Ralph Dawson, one of my dear friends, was driving to work at California State University, Los Angeles, from his beautiful home in Baldwin Hills as he does every day. Employed by the University for 39 years, he was working toward reaching his 40-year mark of employment, in six months. Snapping his fingers to Marvin Gaye while driving down the Santa Monica Freeway, he noticed fog rolling in at a turn he had been making for most of his adult life. The fog appeared thicker than he ever remembered. He glanced down at the console of his Mercedes Benz and noticed fog inside the car as well. He pulled over to the curb because now he couldn't see. He realized this wasn't fog and became frightened. He got on his cell phone and called for help. The notorious "Dr. D," as he is affectionately called, had had a stroke. He said to himself, "Not yet. I have six months to go before retirement. Not yet, dammit! Not yet." Help arrived and took him to Kaiser Permanente Hospital. Sure enough he'd had a stroke.

My friend Clinton Woods and I went to see Ralph and found him lying in a hospital bed, his girlfriend, Sabra, sitting at his side. He greeted us in a low tone, "Woods, Butch (referring to me), how you doin'?" We are all solemn. Clinton and I stepped out when the doctor did his rounds and afterward Ralph gave us the lowdown.

The doctor was recommending that Ralph resign from his job at CSULA and take care of himself. The doctor said the stress was too much for him at his age. This seemed like wise, sound advice. "Damn, man," we both said matter-of-factly.

"Whatcha gon' do?" Ralph said. He told us he was going to give it up and retire, although he voiced concern about the Department of Psychology finding the right person to replace him. We talked back and forth about the importance of health, and I privately had doubts about his giving up a job he loved so much. Clinton and I voiced our concern about Ralph doing the right thing and he assured us both that he was not going back to work.

The following Tuesday, to no one's surprise, Ralph returned to work, running a clinic as busy as it gets with college students and their psychological problems, the kind of stuff that wears on you.

A few of us gave him a call when we heard about his hasty return to work, but he was too busy to talk. The following Saturday we saw him at The Meeting (our regular social gathering) and Woods and I both asked Ralph why he was back at work.

"I told them I am done with work as of October 1, 2008," he said, "my last day."

We both questioned this decision and reminded him that he had just suffered a stroke.

"It's okay," he reassured us. "It's not that big of a deal."

The Meeting is about family. Most of us are in our 60s now and a few are even older. We have supported each other through illness, death, and every catastrophe known to society. We have lost brothers to prostate cancer, heart attack, brain cancer, lung cancer, diabetic comas, and some things we still don't understand. If you want to know something about what's going on, come to The Meeting. (Invitation only.)

Ralph continued to be in a great mood at The Meeting the following week and again casually brushed off our collective concern about his going back to work. One month later, he had another stroke, a mild one this time, probably a TIA. He was out of the hospital before we even knew about it. I visited him at home and wanted to know what was going on. He assured me that everything was okay. What else is there that I can say to him? What concern can I express that has not already been voiced?

Another month went by, another stroke hit, this time more serious than the last. In the hospital he could hardly talk, his voice barely audible, his speech severely impaired. This was serious. His daughter Joi was feeding him and he was gagging. Joi is the gatekeeper of their family. Her presence was reassuring. I was scared to death for my friend.

The doctors moved Ralph to the ICU of a larger hospital better equipped to deal with his stroke. The plan was to put a stent in his neck to assist the blood flow to his brain, a risky procedure, but necessary at this point. Joi explained the procedure to her father, myself, and another mutual friend, Perry Parks. It was successful. The next time I visited, Ralph sounded better—not the same Ralph who could spout words faster than most people can think, but at least an audible Ralph.

This time the decision about returning to work was made for him. The retirement party was planned, and Ralph got the grand send-off on the CSULA campus. Today he is back on his feet, a little shaky, but alive. He will be rehabbing for some time. I would call him hard-headed, except I understand. Lesson learned: Strokes are nothing to play with.

You Have a Higher Risk of Stroke if You:
- Are Black or Hispanic, although Caucasians are at significant risk as well
- Are male
- Have a family history of strokes
- Have had a stroke
- Have high cholesterol
- Are over age 60
- Are severely overweight
- Are a smoker
- Are a heavy drinker of alcohol

HEART ATTACK

A heart attack occurs when the blood supply to the heart muscle is severely reduced or blocked due to blockage in one or more of the coronary arteries. The blockage is usually from the buildup of plaque deposits along the artery walls. The plaque then tears away or ruptures, triggering the formation of a blood clot that blocks the artery and leads to a heart attack.

Most heart attacks happen in the morning. Too often, a heart attack is mistaken as indigestion or heartburn. Be safe and get regular checkups. Know your vitals and whether your blood pressure, cholesterol levels, and Body Mass Index (BMI) are in a healthy range. We know that a lot of what happens to our bodies is hereditary, but most of our individual risk factors can be lowered if we are prudent about how we take care of ourselves.

My friend Rodney was the first person I had known who'd had a heart attack. We grew up together and he was a couple of years behind me in school. A skilled painter, Rodney was the artist of our group. I will never forget the day that Rodney stopped by to visit me in Long Binh, Vietnam, in 1968. He was also serving in the Army and on his way from his base to get some much-needed R&R (rest and relaxation). He had taken a chopper in just to say hello. When you've been in a war zone for a while, the feeling of seeing someone from home is pure joy.

By the mid-'70s, both Rodney and I were living in the California Bay Area. I was working for the 3M Company in South San Francisco and Rodney had his own limousine service in Oakland. He had gained a lot of weight since our days in the Army, and pretty much sat on his butt all day. We discussed his getting into walking and losing some of the weight. I even picked him up from time to time, and we would go walking around Lake Merritt, but it was all for naught. Rodney was a gourmet cook, and eating was as much a hobby as his painting. Cooking, eating, painting, and watching TV made up the recipe for a heart attack. And Rodney eventually had that heart attack.

He was taken to the VA hospital in San Francisco for quadruple bypass surgery. The details of the operation made me quite squeamish. It was too much, having someone pry open your chest. When he came out of recovery, a bunch of his friends and relatives were all standing around his bed, just looking at him, and I guess he knew what we were thinking because he said, "You guys don't understand what it's like to get old." We all laughed except for Rodney's brother, Fred, who said,

"Rodney, you are the youngest in the group." That was a reality check for all of us.

Facts About Heart Attacks

To hear Rodney talk of the pain in his chest was quite disturbing. sometimes heart attacks are described as a feeling of acute indigestion and a compressed feeling in the center of the chest. The actual symptoms to be aware of are:

- Discomfort or pain in the back, neck, jaw, arms, or stomach
- Excessive sweating for no apparent reason, sweaty skin or clammy skin
- Nausea
- Shortness of breath
- Lightheadedness and/or fainting
- Pain in the center of the chest, like you are being squeezed
- An overwhelming tiredness or weakness
- Nervousness and/or unexplained anxiety
- Swelling of the joints, ankles, and lower legs

In recent years women have become more likely to have a heart attack than men. Heart disease is now the leading cause of death in women over the age of 40. As women get older, the risk of heart disease accelerates after menopause, because the body produces less estrogen, and estrogen helps maintain higher levels of good cholesterol and also reduces blood pressure. One in two women will eventually die from heart disease or stroke, compared to one in 30 women that eventually die of breast cancer.

BREAST CANCER

Lumps in the breast aren't the only possible sign of breast cancer, and most breast lumps aren't cancerous. Read about the signs, symptoms, and types of cancer. Generally, breast cancer is seen in women after menopause. But it can strike much earlier. Breast cancer treatments include powerful medicines that can have various side effects. The vast majority of breast cancer patients are women, but every year, about 1,700 U. S. men get breast cancer. Breast cancer symptoms vary widely—from lumps to swelling to skin changes—and many breast cancers have no obvious symptoms at all.

Breast self-exams should be part of a monthly health care routine, and a visit to a doctor if breast changes are experienced. If you're over 40 or at a high risk of the disease, you should also have an annual mammogram and physical exam by a doctor. The earlier breast cancer is found and diagnosed, the better your chances of beating it.

Facts and Myths about Breast Cancer

Myth: All breast lumps are cancerous.

Fact: 8 out of 10 lumps are benign (not cancerous).

Myth: Only women get breast cancer.

Fact: The annual estimate for males who will be diagnosed with breast cancer is 1,700 and the number of men who die from it is 450.

Myth: If your grandmother, mother or sister had breast cancer, you will get it. If no one in your family has had breast cancer, you won't.

Fact: 80 to 85% of women with breast cancer have no family history of the disease.

Myth: Eating high-fat foods causes breast cancer.

Fact: Fatty foods contribute to excess body weight, which is a risk factor. According to the National Cancer Institute: excess body weight increases estrogen production and adds to the level of estrogen in the body. Estrogen stimulates the proliferation of both normal breast cells and cells with cancer-producing DNA mutations.

Myth: Only "old" women get breast cancer.

Fact: 25% of women with breast cancer are younger than 50.

Myth: Breast cancer is a death sentence.

Fact: Up to 98% of women survive at least five years when their cancer is caught early, and 85 to 90% survive at least 10 years.

Myth: If your mammogram is clear, you don't have breast cancer.

Fact: Mammography catches most breast cancers but not all. In addition to mammography, women should have their breasts examined annually by their health care provider and perform monthly breast self-examinations.

Sarah's Story (*I asked Sarah, one of my "angels", to write her story.*) Breast cancer does not care where it strikes, whom it strikes, or whose life it takes. It's tricky; it's unfair; and it's complex. Women over the age of 55 are more likely than younger women to have breast cancer; and a family history of breast cancer, a mother, sister or daughter, may be a factor in a diagnosis. However, according to Mayo Clinic, the majority of people diagnosed with breast cancer have no family history of the disease. Well, in my case, my diagnosis preceded my mother's by three years.

There is so much known about breast cancer, yet there is even more that is unknown. In fact, the cause of breast cancer is still unclear, but what we do know is that it is a horrific demon that not only affects the victim but the victim's family as well.

Just before my 57th birthday, I was visited by the demon, breast cancer. Okay, I was over the age of 55, and I had taken hormone replacement therapy medication, another risk factor. That's only two risk factors.

Breast cancer is tricky. It was not until my mother was 82 that she was diagnosed with breast cancer, and fortunately it was caught between the first and second stage, allowing for a lumpectomy to remove the cancer rather than a mastectomy, a surgical removal of the breast. For me, the cancer was also between the first and second stage, and a lumpectomy performed, but also a lymph node removed, chemotherapy, radiation and an aromatase medication, which was taken for five years post-radiation. The total therapy gave me about a 3% chance of the cancer returning. I am now a 10-year survivor—Thank God!

Breast cancer is unfair, and it can sneak up on you. Now Mom's treatment consisted of the five-year medication alone after her lumpectomy, her age being the determining factor. Then, at the end of the five-year treatment, the demon raised its head again and wreaked havoc in a short period.

Mom was administered a biopsy in September, 2009 and the result was positive for malignancy. This time though, a few months later, Mom was prescribed an oral chemotherapy, rather than the intravenous medication. This was in addition to the 12 other medications she had been taking. Mom suffered with chronic obstructive pulmonary disorder (COPD) as well as congestive heart failure and had recently received a pacemaker implant.

Five months after the second diagnosis, Mom decided not to complete the therapy because she was experiencing its side effects. Plus, even with her Blue Cross and Blue Shield insurance and Medicare, the cost of the medication was huge. It wasn't that Mom could not pay for it; she just didn't want to pay so much for it. And on February 27, 2010 Mom passed away at age 88.

The lesson I learned was that the time may come when I have to decide how long I want to live. It could mean deciding between taking medication and letting time have its way. Mom had known in advance that taking chemotherapy had its side effects, but she wanted to live just a little longer; that was until she heard the cost of the medication, along with suffering the side effects of the chemo. She gave up and refused treatment when it became necessary to be admitted into the hospital. As a result of her refusal of treatment, she passed away. She was ready to say goodbye.

It's not easy, watching someone fight to live; in fact, it's very frustrating, to say the least, and challenging emotionally and physically. Just ask my sister Ann, with whom I shared this experience. Or ask Linda, also a sister, with whom I would discuss the events of Mom's health.

I was aware of the hardship of cancer and the devastation that the therapy could cause. But how can you ask a loved one not to take medication that you know may have serious consequences, when they believe it may prolong their life? If you did ask, would you appear to be asking them to shorten their time? Would you appear to be heartless or uncaring?

There is no manual for how to handle every situation that may arise when caring for a loved one. The least we can do, though, is to educate ourselves, researching solutions to the issues, accompanying the loved one on doctor's visits and into the doctor's office to get first-hand information, for the tough situations will inevitably come. Learning about the health issues of the love one is like being armed for battle.

Breast cancer is complex. There is too much to learn about breast cancer: the types; the signs, symptoms, and causes; the risk factors; the tests and diagnosis; the surgery; the fatigue, coping and needed support; the treatments; and the prevention; therefore, I recommend an article that is available online, *Breast Cancer* by Mayo Clinic staff, to help you prepare to do battle with the demon.

"Where there is no vision, people perish." — PROVERBS 29:18

PROSTATE CANCER

As we all get older, we must be vigilant about health exams. Both men and woman of advancing age should get a checkup annually—women for breast exams and men for prostate exams. Men, in particular, as we get older, will find that our prostate gets larger and as a result will naturally experience many of the symptoms of prostate cancer. That is the reason for the PSA test and the rectal exam, to separate the normal, expected changes from the abnormal ones. The prostate gland is located behind the pubic bone and in front of the rectum. Its primary function is to produce most of the fluids in semen, including the fluid that nourishes and transports sperm. The rectal exam allows the doctor to feel and determine the size of your prostate. There are medicines designed to reduce the size of the prostate, but they have some adverse effects. When a doctor suggested one such drug to me and mentioned that one of the possible side effects was liver damage, I said, "Thank you, Doctor, but I can live with going to the bathroom a couple of times a night. If it gets worse, I will let you know." It is worth repeating: be informed about your choices and treatment options.

Elbert's Story

Elbert Washington, another of my close friends, a high school classmate and fraternity brother, died from prostate cancer. Elbert was an engineer at JPL (Jet Propulsion Laboratory) in Pasadena, California. He had begun having problems with his prostate but ignored them. He said that originally he just had a little difficulty urinating, but then he started urinating frequently and knew that something was really wrong. When it got so bad that he could no longer ignore the discomfort, he went to the doctor and was told that he had prostate cancer. Elbert didn't tell his family. He wanted to go it alone. Finally, the cancer just took over his body. It was too late to do anything else because he had waited too long.

Judge and I visited Elbert in a hospice in Torrance, California. We were so loud that the staff came in and told us to tone it down a notch. We went down memory lane, reminiscing about our high school and college days. Elbert and Judge had attended Long Beach State University together, and they laughed about the days when they used slide rules. I laughed at both, because as they got older, those slide rules got bigger. I called them "the white rulers." Almost simultaneously, the two of them had had an epiphany in their second year of college, that they had to become electrical engineers. When they learned that they could switch their majors to math and be finished with college in one more year instead of three, they both jumped at the opportunity. They talked about it as though they had invented the light bulb!

Elbert was dying, but we laughed and talked for hours on end.

As you might have guessed, Elbert was one of the originals at The Meeting. After he passed, word of his death spread quickly amongst our group. I was hurt, as was everyone who knew him. One Sunday, after a vigorous game of tennis with my brother-in-law Larry, he asked me if I had ever had a prostate test. I answered, "No." Larry spoke to me gruffly and told me that I should get my prostate checked as soon as possible. I was stunned, because we had known each other for almost 30 years and I had never heard him use that tone with me. But I know that he had Elbert on his mind, and it made me feel good to know that he really cared. After tennis on the following Sunday, Larry asked me about getting the test again. That made me say, "Okay, I'll do it."

I scheduled an appointment and went to my doctor to have the prostate-specific antigen (PSA) test and prostate examination performed. Yes, I had to get the exam in which the doctor inserts a gloved finger into the rectum. Yes, it is a very unpleasant experience. But it is a test that I have had every single year for the past 10 years, whether I want to or not. If you are a male over 40 and are wise, you will have the PSA test as well.

Symptoms of Prostate Cancer

- Difficulty urinating, weak or sporadic urine flow
- A sensation that the bladder isn't empty after you are done urinating
- Need to urinate frequently, especially at night (more than twice)

- Pain and burning with urination
- Blood in the urine
- Painful ejaculation
- General pain in the lower back, hips, or upper thighs

WHAT MEN FEAR MOST

More than anything, men fear erectile dysfunction (ED). That's right; they fear that they won't be able to achieve an erection. The facts are that between 25 to 40% of men over 60 years of age have some form of ED. Some of it is due to age, and some of it to prostate treatment. In older men, ED usually has another physical cause, such as disease, injury, or side effects from prescription drugs.

Prescription and over-the-counter drugs can be a problem, and unless you are aware of what you are putting into your body, you could be at risk for adverse effects. Take for instance, prescription drugs like Vioxx. Not enough research was conducted and the drug had to be yanked from the shelves. Why? Because it was found to double the user's risk of heart attack and stroke.

Americans buy more medicine per person than citizens of any other country. About 130 million Americans swallow, gulp, inject, ingest, consume, devour, inhale, and apply patches infused with drugs from 3.5 billion prescriptions written each year. The U.S. is one of only two "advanced" countries on the planet that permits drug advertising on TV!

The more medicine you take, the more likely you are going to have ED. Those are the facts. As a result, the marketplace has exploded with pills to counteract ED. Cialis and Viagra head the list of pills that have made pharmaceutical companies even richer. Any disorder that causes injury to the nerves or impairs blood flow to the penis has the potential to cause ED. I have heard men say that they would rather die than not be able to achieve an erection. Sad commentary. It is also one of the reasons so few men go to the doctor for a regular checkup. Denial? Maybe.

DEMENTIA

The two most common forms of dementia are Alzheimer's disease and multi-infarct dementia (sometimes called vascular dementia). At present, there is no known cure fo either of them. Former President of the United States and California Governor Ronald Reagan suffered from Alzheimer's disease. Near the end of his life, not only was he unable to recognize his own children but he also didn't recognize Nancy Reagan, his wife. President Reagan's final public statement was, "At the moment, I feel just fine. I intend to live the remainder of the years God gives me on this earth doing things I have always done."

Ronald Reagan never had to worry about being institutionalized, but most Alzheimer's patients do, and it is a very difficult decision for families to make. You can expect some resistance from your loved one, and depending on their personality, their resistance could be strong or cursory. If you are in the position of having to decide whether to institutionalize your loved one, you will have to ask yourself some very tough questions. Can I handle my loved one's care on my own? Am I giving him or her the proper care and attention that they need? Is there another family member who is willing and able to step in if I can no longer handle the caregiving? Will my loved one be completely dependent on me? Will I have to bathe, feed, and dress them? Will they need care around the clock?

Alzheimer's disease is most prevalent in people over age 85, although 65 seems to be the early onset age for some. So far most of the studies about Alzheimer's have been on Caucasian patients. As a black man, I have seen a lot of discrimination in my years on the planet. To date, I have seen nothing like what happens to some of our black senior citizens. Older patients are routinely mistreated, undertreated, or overtreated by so-called professionals who have absolutely no training in dealing with older patients suffering from dementia.

Alzheimer's puts loved ones in outer space—lost. Once it starts, it is irreversible. The memory goes, along with any ability to think analytically, or even in the simplest terms. It happens differently for everyone. For example, on the mild end of the spectrum, you might put something down in one place and you spend the rest of the day looking for it. What's worse is that by the time you find it, you forget why you were looking for it. On the extreme end of the spectrum, you aren't able to do simple tasks like dressing, bathing, walking, or even eating.

Warnings Signs of Alzheimer's Disease

- Losing your initiative
- Misplacing things
- Asking the same questions repeatedly
- Inability to follow directions
- Difficulty performing familiar tasks
- Loss of memory that affects job skills
- Difficulty articulating a thought
- Getting disoriented about time, people, and places
- Loss of conceptual thinking
- Poor judgment or lack of judgment
- Erratic behavior, mood, and personality

In its early stages, Alzheimer's can be retarded but not eliminated or "cured." Some of the medications used to calm the symptoms are Exelon, Aricept, Cognexare, and Reminyl—but they only create a delay in the progression of the disease. The FDA (Food and Drug Administration) is developing other medications that are supposed to help slow the disease. However, it is my feeling that as long as the drug companies can make a dollar, some kind of drug will be out there for you to take. I suggest caution when consuming these drugs.

The holistic approach to treatment seems to be the most trustworthy. Simple actions, involving no drugs, have been shown to help keep the brain sharp. Control the blood pressure of the patient. Exercise their mind by playing games with them. Chess and scrabble are good games to keep them thinking and analyzing. Reading and writing are also stimulating activities. If your loved one ever played a musical instrument in the past, getting them back to it could be beneficial. Mentally stimulating activities will do more good than pills. Additionally, good nutrition is a crucial part of the holistic approach to treating Alzheimer's patients. Vitamins A and E, along with leafy green vegetables seem to be effective nutrients.

OSTEOPOROSIS

Osteoporosis literally means "porous bones." It is a disease in which the amount of bone is decreased, the strength of the spongy interior of the bone is reduced, and the surface of the bone becomes thin, making them susceptible to fractures. In seniors, typical fractures occur in the spine, hip and wrist, because of osteoporosis.

The collapse of vertebrae leads to chronic pain and the characteristic bent spine, or "hunchback," while fractures of the larger bones impair mobility and may require surgery. Hip fractures, in particular, can result in permanent disability. It is estimated that more than 10 million Americans have established osteoporosis, and another 34 million have osteopenia, or low bone mass, which is the precursor to osteoporosis, responsible for 1.5 million fractures annually. About 50% of women and 25% men are expected to have osteoporosis in their lifetime, according to the National Osteoporosis Foundation.

Osteoporosis is sometimes called "the silent disease" because the bone loss occurs without symptoms. It is only after a sudden bump or fall, causing a fracture or a vertebrae collapse, that it is realized that you have the disease. If you have ever seen that old man or woman, who is hunched over and can't seem to straighten up, then you've seen kyphosis (stooped shoulder), one of the deformities resulting from osteoporosis.

What Can Be Done to Prevent Osteoporosis?

There are treatments available for those suffering from osteoporosis, but there is no cure. Prevention is the key: staying physically active, eating a variety of whole plant foods, avoiding animal foods, including dairy products, and keeping salt intake to a minimum. Regular weight-bearing exercise and simply walking are excellent for prevention. Avoid tobacco, alcohol, and caffeine, but consume the daily recommended amounts of calcium and Vitamin D and take a daily multivitamin as extra "insurance."

Risk Factors for Osteoporosis

- Being of advanced age
- Having a thin and/or small body frame
- Being female

- Having a family history of osteoporosis
- Being post-menopausal, including surgically-induced menopause
- Consuming insufficient calcium
- Being Caucasian
- Being anorexic
- Living an inactive lifestyle

IN SUMMARY

A key factor in health care is having regular checkups. Be prudent about your own health. Understand what you are putting in your body. Recognizing health issues will be a full-time job. You can bet, as we all get older, we are going to have some of the symptoms mentioned in this chapter. The list includes the most common, and ones you should be aware of—know how to provide comfort. Preventive care is the best bet—we all will travel this route.

WISE TIPS

Take care of yourself by modeling those of your age who are healthy. Yoga, meditating, and Tai Chi are keys to helping you stay fit mentally and physically. There are many resources available to you, and most of them are at your fingertips. Use them.

CAREGIVING QUOTES

My family lives together, and we take care of each other. My mother, sister and three brothers all live together. My oldest brother had some mental problems, and we take care of him here at home. We are family, and that is the way it should be.

— JACY GOMES, COSTELLO BRANCO, Salvador, Brazil

"When a person has manifested a disease in the body temple or some kind of discomfort in their life, can it be turned around through the power of 'right' thinking?" And the answer is absolutely, yes.
— REV. MICHAEL BERNARD BECKWITH —

CHAPTER 8
Visiting the Hospital

"Never expose yourself unnecessarily to danger, a miracle may not save you...and if it does, it will be deducted from your share of luck or merit."

— THE TALMUD

AT SOME POINT in their lives, 1 in 10 Americans will be a patient in a hospital. The number for seniors is even higher. Now more than ever, it is necessary to know what to expect when you go to the hospital. The healthcare industry has been transitioning since the turn of the century, and the driving force for hospitals has become the insurance companies. Insurance companies have even pressed for fewer medical exams and shorter hospital stays.

Of course, it is always best to try to stay out of the hospital altogether, and that applies to us, the caregivers, as well as our loved ones. If a visit to the hospital is unavoidable, however, it is always best to be prepared.

If a doctor has recommended surgery for your loved one, **have him explain why** it is needed, and prepare a hospital checklist.

Is the surgery really needed? That should be the first question you ask. Selecting the hospital is also important. The doctor or surgeon will want to send you to the hospital where they have operating privileges. Your loved one's medical insurance may want to send you to the hospital that charges the least amount of money. The truth is, some hospitals are better than others. Some have better records of success, and some provide a better atmosphere. Be an informed consumer and check it all out for yourself.

The checklist should include these items:

- Get a second opinion.
- Meet the surgeon ahead of time and take notes.

- Find out the hospital's success rate with the procedure being performed.
- Give the anesthesiologist your loved one's complete medical history.
- Discuss any allergic reactions in advance.
- Know who will be in charge of the hospital stay at every stage.
- Sign advanced directives after treatment options are fully understood.
- Pack a list of phone numbers that might be needed in an emergency.
- Keep accurate records, starting with the diagnosis, in case of a problem with billing or insurance.
- Plan for recovery care before being admitted.

FAMILY ADVOCACY

The hospital near Mom's home in Los Angeles was Brotman Medical Center in Culver City, located across the street from Sony Pictures Studios. Brotman received a great deal of news exposure years ago, when pop superstar Michael Jackson donated millions of dollars to its burn center after they treated him for injuries he suffered during the filming of a Pepsi commercial. Because of Mom's strokes, she was a frequent guest at Brotman. For her, it was the TIAs that would come and go. One minute Mom would be talking, and the next minute her face was a blank stare with a frozen expression on her face. I can remember saying to her softly, "Mama? Mama?," my hands gently holding her face. The first time Mom had a TIA in my presence, I was horrified. It wasn't the sight of it, but my feeling of helplessness. The symptoms of TIA generally go away within 24 hours. I would always call 911 for an ambulance, and Mom would be transported directly to Brotman.

On one of my visits to see Mom, there were at least 18 people who had formed a picket line outside of the hospital entrance. Brotman has an excellent history of taking care of elderly patients, but on this day there were picket signs. One sign had a picture of a woman, and the other signs said, "Brotman killed our Mother." After the third day of seeing them protest, I stopped and asked the family for some details on what had been an obvious catastrophe.

As it was told to me, their mother had died at Brotman on a Friday, and no one had been available to take her remains to the refrigerated morgue. Her body became badly swollen, and the family had not been notified until the following Tuesday evening. Understandably, the family was up in arms about the mistreatment of their mother. Why had it taken so long for the hospital to contact them? They went on to say that the hospital was going to have hell to pay. The family had retained a lawyer and was preparing to file suit against Brotman for neglect.

I discussed what I had learned about the situation with my sister Maggie who was with me at the time. I asked her, "What's wrong with this picture?" Maggie looked at me curiously and responded, "I don't know, but it looks like the hospital screwed up pretty bad though." She was right, the hospital had screwed up pretty badly, but so had that family. In my opinion, the other part of the picture was that no one from the deceased woman's family had been at the hospital for at least five days, perhaps longer. If the family had visited the hospital regularly, perhaps that particular tragedy would never never have happened. Who had looked out for the woman on a daily basis? How was it possible that no one knew what was going on? Was her death sudden? What was the cause? Did she have an adverse reaction to a medication or treatment? Was she given the wrong medication?

Now it was becoming clearer why I had accepted the responsibility of scheduling family members to visit Mom on different days in the hospital. I don't mean to suggest that gathering the family and having them agree on anything are easy tasks! They're not. But what must be understood is that hospitals across the country are concerned with their bottom line. The average length of time that a patient stays in the hospital is much shorter now than it has ever been, and the hospital staff is not what it used to be. In some cases, I encountered language barriers when communicating with some of the nursing staff. How can you be sure you are meeting the needs of your patients if you cannot fully understand each other?

Almost any hospital that you visit will show some form of neglect, especially towards elderly patients. It is not unusual to see your loved one restrained and bound to a wheelchair. The very first time I saw my mother in that position I was outraged and demanded that they untie her. Since Mom was forever trying to get up and go to the bathroom on her own, it provided enough justification to restrain her to prevent her from hurting herself. However, that type of treatment is also a sign of a short staff. When Mom was discharged, we never returned to that particular hospital.

After numerous meetings our family did a great job of visiting Mom on the days that they could. The hospital saw someone different in Mom's room almost every day. Some family members would visit in the morning, others would visit during their lunch hour. The most popular time was after work. All the nurses at the station knew Mom by name and directed visitors to her room without hesitation.

Having a strong family presence is also a safeguard against neglect. Every family member was instructed to ask questions of the nurses and doctors who were on duty. Visitors would also bring candy, cards, and little gifts to the nursing staff as well, signed "From the family of Mary Jacquet Simmons." The idea of having someone from the family present at the hospital all of the time is a proactive stance—it lets the staff know that this patient has people who care about them, and those people are looking over the staff's shoulders. This stance also makes it less likely that there will be mishaps or, heaven forbid, neglect. In addition to visiting, I would also call the hospital every single day just to check on Mom's status. It's only a two-minute exercise, and it's another reminder to the staff that the family cares—and is watching.

Remember that persistence pays. Since I took the responsibility as the "family gatekeeper," I also took on the responsibility of promoting a higher level of recuperation for Mom. Assertiveness pays off, while timid compliance is often rewarded with slower and less vigilant care. When people don't advocate for themselves, they don't always receive the care that they are entitled to. That's why it is important for patients to have a competent family advocate to improve the whole experience and shorten the care process. Family advocacy also improves the patient's overall sense of wellbeing and safety. My advantage as an advocate comes, in part, by spending over 30 years in the sometimes nasty and competitive corporate arena of sales and management and, more importantly, living to tell about it.

The first thing that a family advocate must do is become informed. If a medical procedure is recommended, ask why it is needed and how it works? Find out what the alternative treatments are, if any. Know who will administer the treatment and the aftercare. Know what medications are being administered, how much and how often, what they're for, and what the possible side effects are. Make sure that you ask what you can do to help.

Becoming knowledgeable about your loved one's medications is one aspect of care that is often neglected, because we assume that the staff knows everything about what's going on. They don't! There are medication mishaps more often than you would think. It is not uncommon for patients to be given the wrong dosage, or to receive medication at the wrong time. Sometimes medication is even given to the wrong patient!

ADVERSE EVENTS OF MEDICATION

Medication mishaps can happen to anyone whether they have family advocates or not, whether rich or poor, famous or unknown. In November of 2007, actor Dennis Quaid and his wife, Kimberly, had twins via a surrogate. The children were given overdoses of a blood thinning medication at Cedars-Sinai Medical Center, arguably the most prestigious hospital in Southern California. The Quaid twins were being treated for a staph infection, and they almost died. Why? A technician mistook an "a" for an "o" in a drug name. A doctor misplaced a decimal point in a prescription order. A nurse reached for a vial of medicine in a cabinet, as she had done hundreds of times before, only this time the light was dim and she failed to notice that the label was sky-blue and not powder-blue. Slip-ups are often simple, always human, and have happened in hospitals as well as homes.

"It's never just one thing that goes wrong when a serious event happens," says Michael Cohen, president of the Institute for Safe Medication Practices. "We've detailed a situation where we found over 50 mistakes in the system before an infant was killed." The incident, according to Mr. Cohen, was a 1,000-fold overdose of the blood thinner heparin in an Indianapolis neonatal intensive care unit that resulted in the deaths of three infants in 2006. It was the exact thing that happened to the Quaid twins. "The pharmacy dispensed the wrong dose to the nursing station," Cohen said.

If the care being given doesn't fit your expectations, question it. If the medication is one that you haven't seen your loved one receive before, ask who ordered it. If the staff does not know, make sure that they check to verify. I don't mean to be cynical, because you do have to have some faith. But if your mom had been getting a blue pill each day, then suddenly it's a red pill, you would ask if it's the *right* pill before it is given. Don't worry that you might be a pain to the staff. Hospitals are used to dealing with sleep-deprived, anxiety-ridden, crazed family members. Offending the staff should be the least of your worries.

Dr. Harold H. Benjamin, the founder of "The Wellness Community," a nationwide network of psychosocial support groups for cancer patients and their families, shares in his book, *From Victim to Victor*, that most doctors, because of their training, have a difficult time interacting with patients other than as a parental figure. The physicians who view themselves this way are less likely to share the responsibility of care, discuss treatment options, or answer questions and accept input from patients and their caregivers. Instead, they are used to giving orders and having others simply follow them. They may also be brusque, use confusing medical jargon, and interrupt the patient or caregiver as he or she discloses important information.

In a study with professional caregivers in New York, one of the social workers said, "We are professionals, and we study this [dealing with sick people and their families] and see this all the time, and we can't help but to sometimes feel superior." If a social worker feels superior, you know damn well a doctor probably does.

Dr. Lucien Leape is one of the authors of a 1999 Institute of Medicine report that estimated 100,000 people die each year in the U.S. from *preventable* hospital errors. Dr. Leape states, "People used to say that hospital mistakes are kind of like the poor—they're always with you." The mid-1990s saw a rash of medical errors that caught the attention of the public, and the medical profession. For instance, a Florida man had the wrong leg amputated; a New York woman had surgery on the wrong side of her brain; and Betsy Lehman, a newspaper reporter who covered the health beat, died of an accidental chemotherapy overdose at one of the nation's top cancer centers, Boston's Dana Farber Cancer Center. Initially, the Center's error was covered up by the American Medical Association as some rare mistake. The AMA later changed its stance, admitting that such errors were "common."

In the state of California, 1,002 incidents of medical mistakes were disclosed between July 2007 and May 2008. The disclosures were the first set under a state law that requires hospitals to inform health regulators of all substantial injuries to patients. The official name for such incidents is "adverse events," but they are also known as: "never events." Why? Because they are considered preventable by the safety experts and should never happen.

Despite this law, hospital patients in California are being injured substantially at a rate of 100 per month, according to data compiled by the California State Department of Health. Beth Capell, a lobbyist for Health Access California (a consumer group), says, "I think the 'never events' are a wake-up call to everyone about the safety of California hospitals."

Even Dr. Donald Berwick, the president of the Institute for Healthcare Improvement (a Massachusetts nonprofit) said the number of mistakes is certainly higher than what California hospitals have recently disclosed. His estimate is that 15 million patients are harmed each year in hospitals. Fifteen million! That is downright scary. Dr. Berwick said, "It will always be true that the vast majority of incidents are never reported."

Here is a sample of what *was* reported by 518 California hospitals. There were:

- **466** bedsores (advanced skin ulcers). Some patients developed bedsores so severe that the dead skin formed a crater or rotted through to the muscle or bone. Many times these are the same patients that are being restrained by belts.
- **145** objects left in the patient after surgery. These patients had foreign objects like surgical equipment left inside their bodies.
- **34** died while under anesthesia.
- **41** surgeries in which doctors performed the wrong procedure, or operated on the wrong body part, or on the wrong patient. How can this be?

- **44** restraint techniques that caused either death or disability. Theoretically, these should be included in the bedsores category. From my research and personal observation, the use of restraints is the most inhumane treatment in existence. I am of the opinion that surely, there must be a better method.
- **43** sexual assaults on patients. This is the only thing worse than restraints. This behavior has the Marquis de Sade taking a back seat. God help us.

Dr. Angela Scioscia of the UC San Diego Medical Center said, "We don't want people to be afraid when they come into hospitals, because they are becoming safer and safer all the time." Well, Dr. Scioscia, I think we should be scared out of our pants, and we should have our family checking every single detail to ensure our safety. As a matter of fact, it would be prudent to bring along a tape recorder. The weird part of this is that the hospitals get paid whether they do a good job or not. Why is that? I have been made aware that some legislation was introduced in California to make hospitals accountable. Assemblyman Mike Feuer (D-Los Angeles) proposed that medical providers be barred from seeking payment on "adverse events" and the bill is currently being rewritten. Good luck, Assemblyman Feuer. I am happy that someone has acknowledged the fear factor of going into the hospital. The truth is, 100,000 deaths a year is a conservative number; some even say that it is twice that. That's more deaths by mistake than deaths caused by breast cancer, AIDS, and motor vehicle accidents combined.

Doctors and other healthcare professionals are affected by their mistakes. A survey of more than 3,000 doctors in the August 2007 Joint Commission Journal on Quality and Patient Safety, found that doctors lost confidence, were anxious about future errors, and had trouble sleeping. Frankly, I don't give a damn. And neither should you. I say, "Do your job, doctor. I'm looking over your shoulder, and I'm taking notes."

BE AN INFORMED CONSUMER

Dr. Peter Angood is a trauma surgeon and Vice President and Chief Patient Safety Officer for the Joint Commission on Accreditation of Healthcare Organizations (JCAHO), a national organization that accredits hospitals and other healthcare facilities. Dr. Angood states, "There's an assumption that hospitals should have all the information and you should just take at face value what the hospitals tell you. One of the biggest things we can do in healthcare is to help patients understand that they need to be better consumers. It's good to question, to ask for clarification, and solicit second opinions as needed."

Three of my friends have had heart surgery in recent years. Only one of them really needed it. Two had their surgeries performed at Veterans Administration (VA) Hospitals, and the other at a top hospital in Massachusetts. One is suing his hospital for unnec- essary surgery, and the other two are going on about their lives. Not one of them thought to get a second opinion. Why? Is it because we have been programmed not to question the opinions of doctors?

A group called The American Medical Consumers is aware of the medical errors that exist. They conducted a telephone survey of over 2,000 randomly selected adults in 2005 called the National Survey on Consumers' Experiences with Patient Safety and Quality Information (a joint project with Harvard School of Public Health and Kaiser Family Foundation). Of those surveyed:

- 48% were concerned about the safety of medical care.
- 34% had experienced a medical error, or a family member had.
- 92% believed serious medical errors should be reported.
- 63% believed medical error reports should be made public.
- 69% had double-checked that a drug they got from a pharmacy is the same as their doctor prescribed.
- 48% had taken a list of medications to their doctor visits.
- 69% had called to check results of medical tests.
- 43% had brought a support person to a medical appointment.

In spite of these statistics, there are steps you can take for yourself and your loved one when a hospital stay is necessary. They include these twelve simple ways to feel empowered:

1. Don't let intimidation keep you from asking questions.
2. Get your own support system in place.
3. Bring a pencil and pad to the hospital to write things down. (It's okay to bring a tape recorder, too.)
4. Note people's names.

5. Bring in family pictures.
6. Emotionally connect with someone who works in the hospital.
7. Keep a journal.
8. Verify that every caregiver is providing the right service.
9. When therapy is in process, ask what you can learn to reinforce treatments.
10. Share tips with the staff on your loved one's needs and preferences.
11. Bring in your favorite foods instead of relying on the cafeteria.
12. Get plenty of sleep.

"We are guests in our patients' lives; and we are their host when they come to us. Why should they, or we, expect anything less than the graciousness expected by guests and from hosts at their very best. Service is quality."

— DR. DONALD BERWICK, Administrator for the Centers for Medicare and Medicaid Services, 2011

STAY OUT OF THE HOSPITAL, IF YOU CAN

Lloyd's Story

Kaiser Permanente in West Los Angeles has a great location right off of the Santa Monica Freeway, and a reputation for providing great care. On November 17, 2002, I received an urgent phone call from my brother-in-law, Larry, to let me know that one of our dear friends had been admitted at Kaiser. "What happened?" I asked. Larry said, "He was taken to the hospital last night and he is in a coma. It doesn't look good." I got to the hospital as quickly as I could and when I arrived, our friend's room was full of "the fellas from The Meeting." We all gathered around his bed and joined in prayer.

Lloyd Linsey, a.k.a. "Double L," and Larry share a long history from their college years at UCLA. They were among the few "brothas" on campus when Kareem Abdul Jabbar (then Lew Alcindor) arrived as a freshman. It is a time in history over which the two of them often reminisce with glee. "Double L" is normally the proverbial "life of the party," but on this night he had tubes, monitors, and needles coming from all over his body. The sight of a brother who is always so full of energy lying there in a coma was a shock and a reminder of life's fragility. I thought back to Larry's words to me on the phone earlier that night: "It doesn't look good."

A few of us retired to the waiting room. It was unspoken but understood that Larry would be the one from our group who would work with Karen, "Double L's" wife, to handle whatever arrangements became necessary. He was our brother, an original from The Meetings, and we would all do whatever needed to be done.

Some 20 minutes later, Karen returned to the waiting room and informed us that one of the doctors wanted to talk to her, and she needed support. We followed her into a private room; the lighting was somewhat subdued. There were seven of us in that room to support our brother's wife. The doctor, who was female and of East Indian descent, wasted no time in getting to the point. She said to Karen, "I want your permission to take your husband off life support."

Karen looked up at the doctor, who was sitting upright but for some reason seemed to be sitting higher than everyone else. Karen said, "No" without hesitation. It was an emphatic "No" and we all understood it. The doctor then said, "Your husband is not going to pull through this," and proceeded to explain all of the complications associated with his coma. She reiterated the request to take "Double L" off life support, seemingly suggesting that it would be nonsensical to do otherwise. Karen leaned on Larry, who is an attorney, and as if talking through him, said, "I don't want my husband taken off life support." The doctor's tone seemed misplaced as she asked for the third time, but was cut off in mid-sentence by Karen, with a stern and final "No."

The doctor got up and walked out of the room without another word. The other Lloyd in our group, Lloyd Ferguson, exchanged words with Larry as they both acknowledged the audacity and apathetic tone of the doctor. It was as if she were saying, "How dare you question me?" Karen thanked us for being in the room with her for support. We shared a group hug and talked about the lack of respect we had just been shown.

"Double L"'s friends and family were in and out of the hospital for the next three days. On Thursday morning, the fourth day, I got the word that "Double L" had opened his eyes. He was out of the coma. On Friday, he was talking. He was still weak, but soon he was well enough to move to a rehab center and after two months he was back at home. His body had atrophied, and he had a tough time getting around. He couldn't drive yet, but he was back to his old self within a few months. Today, he is enjoying his retirement.

"Double L" learned that his coma was a result of a diabetic attack, so he changed his diet considerably. He now eats only the best nutritional foods, he takes his medication on a timely basis, and avoids anything toxic entering his body. His life is now more regimented. Exactly one year after falling into his coma, "Double L" gave himself an "anniversary party" at Larry's, the most popular Jamaican restaurant in Los Angeles. The invitation read: "Lazarus returns from the dead." We all rejoiced at that moment in time. He had his tenth anniversary of recovery in 2012.

IN SUMMARY

You must take on the responsibility of advocate for your loved one. Don't be afraid to ask questions of doctors. We are in a new information age—and we communicate at such a higher level. Believe me, they are weary of tweets, photo phones, and Facebook. Coordinate visiting hours and days with the hospital—and share it with the family.

WISE TIPS

If you are sick with a cold or the flu, stay home. If you are not feeling well, stay home. Hospital patients are at a higher risk of infection. Make a phone call instead. Visit when you are feeling better. When you arrive at the hospital, wash your hands. Put your cell phone on vibrate or turn it off. Staying too long on the visit will often tire the patient. Use common sense; you are visiting to show support.

"What lies before us, what lies behind us, are nothing compared to what lies within us."
— RALPH WALDO EMERSON

CHAPTER 9
Choosing a Residential Care Facility

"God speaks whenever He finds a humble, listening ear. And the language He uses is kindness."

— LENA HORNE

GETTING MY MOTHER released from the nursing home with little challenge was truly a triumph. I am aware that entering a nursing home is a fear for many seniors. The moment you walk into a nursing home or care facility you see the sick, mostly elderly, people in hallways and in beds. Unless you have a lot of money so that income is not an issue, you are at risk. Unfortunately, we are in an era where money rules.

While I believed a nursing home was not an option for my mother, there may come a time when others must make a different choice. Nursing homes can mean the complete loss of independence and the last stop before death for some seniors, and we have all heard enough horror stories about some of them. If a nursing home becomes the best choice for your loved one, there are things to keep in mind in order to take everyone's feelings into consideration.

For the senior entering the nursing home, it means that most or all of the little possessions they treasured are left behind. The privacy of home and its familiar surroundings soon become a distant memory. Sociologists liken it to prison, where you have no control over eating, sleeping, and everyday activities. The routine of the senior is changed forever, and the loss of certainty and familiarity brings about anxiety. It means they have entered a phase very similar to their childhood, when they entered nursery school or kindergarten for the first time. They may not have the words to describe their feelings but we should realize that they are frightened. They are feeling vulnerable and afraid of what lies ahead.

For the caregiver, there may be feelings of giving up or giving in, even if the decision to place your loved one in a nursing home is one of financial or medical necessity. Sometimes the therapy for a loved one's needs cannot be performed at home; sometimes it is impossible for the caregiver to perform even the slightest of caring duties. Whatever the case, a nursing home or assisted living facility should be chosen with the best of care.

WHAT IS ASSISTED LIVING?

"Assisted living" is a non-medical, residential long-term care facility for elders that can no longer live alone for any number of reasons. Most usually these are issues that are called ADLs ("activities of daily living"), like bathing, dressing, grooming, toileting, eating, and/or physical disabilities. What most do not need is "acute medical care" that requires daily maintenance or treatment, although some assisted living homes have that (and hospice) capacity as well. All manage medications and diet, provide transportation, housekeeping, and laundry services, and are monitored regularly by state or local officials.

Particularly in the small group home setting, assisted living has been likened to a relative caring for elder parents or grandparents. The smaller the home, the more personal, individualized, and accommodating it can be.

However, while assisted living tends to be less costly and more hospitable than nursing homes, it is not necessarily covered by Medicare or Medicaid. What to look for when choosing a residential facility, however, is the same for both.

CHOOSING A NURSING OR ASSISTED LIVING HOME

Choosing a residential care home is something that takes a great deal of planning. Frequently, the decision is made in a hurry. For instance, your loved one is just released from the hospital and needs a place for physical therapy. Where do you take them? Usually, a nursing home is the first place that comes to mind. Today, the options are many. Take the time beforehand to look into what is available for the recovery and therapy your loved one needs. Generally, when you rush, you make uninformed choices. Do your own research. Many times, when a hospital or provider gives a recommendation, it is because they have some sort of business connection to that particular facility. My suggestion is to get everyone in the family involved in the decision. If there is no family member who steps up to take care of your loved one, then you want to do the next best thing.

Start off by making a list of residential "long term care" facilities homes in your area. In Los Angeles, there are so many nursing homes that the only trouble deciding on one will be ascertaining the quality of care it provides. Gather information about facilities from their in-house or state ombudsmen, if they have one. The key is to visit the homes or your local Area Office on Aging to see them for yourself. Ideally, the facility will be one that is chosen and agreed upon by the people geographically closest to your loved one. The closer your loved one is to their family, the greater the possibility of visitors he or she will have. And the more the visitors, the better the care. That is just human nature. Beyond that, figure out what the restrictions are in terms of cost.

The average national cost of full-time care in a nursing or large assisted living facility is close to $60,000.00 a year. So, if your loved one has Medicare or Medicaid you will want to check and see which facilities accept it. Make a list of at least five homes that you want the family to evaluate. Like any other major decision or investment, you want to compare one against the other.

WHAT TO LOOK FOR IN A RESIDENTIAL CARE FACILITY HOME

Some obvious things that any home should have are a current operating license from the state, certification under Medicare or Medicaid (if either will be used to help cover the costs), copies of their most recent inspection reports, and adequate staffing. In addition to these minimum requirements, you should also look for the following:

- Check for cleanliness from the front of the facility to the back. Are the floors clean in the entry area and hallways? What about the patients' rooms? What about the bathrooms?
- Are there strong odors in the air? Smells are telltale signs of good or bad care.

- What is the resident dining room like? Is it clean? Does the facility provide a balanced diet? How does the food taste? Make an unannounced visit at meal time.
- Is there an active resident council and posted Bill of Rights?
- Do the residents look well cared for, clean, and appropriately dressed for daily activities?
- Are the residents treated with respect? Is the staff friendly and patient? Ask how they handle the patients who are incontinent, and those with dementia.
- What is their philosophy on restraints?
- Are the residents being engaged or participating in activities? Is there a posted schedule of daily activities or events so that everyone knows what is going on?
- Is there equipment for rehabbing? Do the residents have opportunities for physical activity? Are they ever taken outside for fresh air?
- Do the patients' bedrooms open onto a corridor where they can be easily seen and heard in an emergency? Do they have windows?
- Are there any volunteer programs in place? Volunteers can read to the patients, entertain them, or possibly assist with a movie night.
- Is transportation provided for appointments or activities?

As you evaluate what is available in your city, consider the accommodations and safety. How many residents share a bathroom? Can they bring in their own furniture and/or decorate their rooms? Do they have guest accommodations? Is there security on duty 24 hours a day? Is a nurse available around the clock? What happens in case of an emergency or natural disaster? What are the evacuation procedures?

As you complete your research and begin narrowing your choices, try to visit every home on your short list. You will want to talk to everyone in the facility, from the director to the staff.

Check out the numerous resources on the internet. You will find plenty of referral services and paid professionals, who will gather information for you. The caveat is that they get paid on your accepting their recommendations, so you must physically inspect each place and make the comparisons. Ask to speak with the Director at each center.

Generally, they will take you on a tour of the facility and answer all of your questions. Weekends or evenings is a good time to visit. This way, you can get an idea of what to expect during peak hours when there are lots of visitors and activity.

When you observe other families present, don't be afraid to ask them questions. They will be the most candid. That is one of the truest tests in choosing the right place. If you can, talk with some of the residents as well.

IDENTIFYING POOR CARE IN A RESIDENTIAL FACILITY

- Are restraints used? Wheelchair bars used? Restricti vests? Do they use lap trays that are locked and/or devices that force people to stay in their beds and wheelchairs? These devices are both dangerous and demeaning, and generally mean that the place is understaffed or the staff is poorly trained, underpaid, and unqualified.
- Are the smells of urine, feces, or other odors unmistakable?
- Does the staff assist the patients with eating?
- Does the staff respond to calls for help?
- Does the staff "talk down" to residents? Are they being treated roughly or disrespectfully?
- Do the residents have privacy? Are they partially clothed in the hallway? Does staff just walk in on them while they are dressing?
- Are the patients clumped in one area doing nothing? Boredom, inactivity, and loneliness are more signs of poor care.

LONG TERM CARE RESIDENTS DO HAVE RIGHTS

The image of restraints is stuck in my head, since my mother was subjected to their use in the nursing home. Years later, I would see my Aunt Eva restrained in a wheelchair in the hallway of her nursing home, and my heart still aches from that memory. I didn't know then what I know now—seniors have rights, and they have avenues to advocates who will intervene on their behalf. The state long-term care ombudsmen are put into place specifically to report abuse and/ or neglect in nursing homes and other senior care facilities. They have investigated more than 285,000 complaints and have provided useful and helpful information to close to a half-million people.

The Ombudsmen program is now operating in all 50 states with a staff of over 1,300 paid ombudsmen and 13,000 certified volunteer ombudsmen, working in 600 locations nationwide. The program started in 1972 as a demonstration program. Today, it is in all states under the Older Americans Act, which is administered by the Administration on Aging (AoA). Thousands of trained volunteer ombudsmen regularly visit long-term care facilities and monitor the conditions.

Ombudsmen help seniors exercise the rights that are guaranteed to them by law. The problem is that the senior population is growing so fast, and very few people even know that ombudsmen exist. I have asked a number of seniors about ombudsmen and gotten a blank stare in response. What are the rights of those in senior care facilities, board and care homes, and assisted living facilities? For starters, residents should be free of physical restraints; be able to voice grievances without fear of retaliation; be able to send and receive personal mail; be treated with respect and dignity; be able to communicate privately with anyone they choose; and have medical records kept confidential.

IN SUMMARY

Having your loved one at home will help you monitor their condition. This is what you may not be assured of in a nursing or assisted living home. Monitoring a loved one's eating, drinking, and sleeping habits will help you know the type of medical help they need. When they are at home with you, you have peace of mind. Think carefully about putting a loved one in a nursing home, especially. Of course, it is not an easy decision to make. It generally concerns the entire family. Weigh all the pros and cons—many caregivers are at risk. Can you handle the job of a caregiver? Shop around before you make the decision.

WISE TIPS

Every day, people are faced with finding residential care for themselves or someone they love. Your individual needs will require individual planning. Make sure the family is involved in the process as much as possible. Understand your options and learn as much as possible to make the choice. Over 70% of nursing home residents receive help from Medicaid.

CAREGIVING QUOTES
(On the Subject of Restraints)

I speak as a former nursing home care administrator. In nursing home care for the elderly and/or disabled, nothing is worse than walking into a facility with a foul odor, limited staff and patients sitting around listlessly, some restrained to their seats and beds. In our world, it was against patients' rights to be restrained to their seats and beds. In our world, it was against patients' rights to be restrained, either chemically (excessive medication) or physically. Restorative Therapy Aides (RTAs) would help residents with their exercise schedules as prescribed by physical therapists. Low beds without side rails were used. If a patient "fell" out of bed, he/she would simply roll onto a padded mat placed on the floor beside the bed. These practices are used by facilities that are committed to providing the safest, most restraint- free environment possible.

— CLAIRE ACRE, 57, Salt Lake City, Utah

I am a caregiver to a quadriplegic man here in Fresno, California. The subject of restraints is very touchy for me. I think restraints are wrong. This very topic hurts my heart. It's humiliating and degrading. We are a great nation, so how is it possible that we are running care facilities like cave men? Some patients can cause harm to the staff and to themselves. But restraints are not the answer. We must find a better solution.

— AURORA GARCIA, 41, Fresno, CA

As a caregiver from the Philippines, living in Israel, I have observed many patients who need to be restrained. Especially when they are going wild. Some patients need restraints when they are getting dialysis treatments. So their hands are tied to avoid problems. Some social workers are patient and some are not. I treat my patients like they are at home.

— LINDA QUEVADA, 55, Israel

"Who can protest and does not is an accomplice in the act."
— THE TALMUD

CHAPTER 10
Understanding Medicare and Medicaid

The ancestor of every action is a thought."
— RALPH W. EMERSON

ONE GOOD THING about being old is that you've made it to an age where age is a concern. According to many actuarial charts, few people of color are expected to live beyond 55 years of age. If you are a person of color and have reached age 55, you have already made it to a place where few arrive, such as my mother, who died at 82 years of age and for most of her life lived pretty healthily. She had periods when she would gain a lot of weight and was in her sixties when she finally got a handle on eating to relieve stress. My father, on the other hand, died at 50 years of age, five years short of expectations.

What is waiting for those who survive the misdeeds of a society that places so much value on the color of one's skin? The answer to that question will face much greater resistance since Barack Obama became President of the United States. Talk about setting the bar high! He was aware of what is going on with the healthcare crisis in our country and he vowed throughout his campaign that repairing the healthcare system would be one of his top priorities as President. Politics being what it is, creating a new healthcare system has been as easy as pulling a tree out of the ground. (See Affordable Care Act on page 120.)

The way some seniors are treated is downright awful—and if you are a senior of color, you can expect even more contempt. I speak from the experience of following up on a number of incidents and situations involving my mother in her senior years and further research I conducted after her death in 1997. And, of course, there are hundreds of stories of the mistreatment of whites as well. Healthcare and its abuses have become a national pandemic.

Many so-called "government services" are, in my opinion, some of the biggest known rip-offs. In-Home Supportive Services (IHSS) is one of those bureaucratic operations that supposedly exist to assist seniors. IHSS is run by the Health and Welfare Agency Department of Social Services and is designed to provide money for a nurse or part- time caregiver to assist the senior in their home.

It is difficult to communicate with IHSS, but if you are persistent enough you might get to speak with them on the phone. I say persistent, because I personally spent over two weeks just to get them to answer the phone. If I had a tough time, then I can only assume that most people will never be able to contact them. If and when you finally do get someone on the phone, it will be another month before someone will come out to visit your loved one and assess their needs. That is a fact in Los Angeles. I know several people who have had the same experience.

After the assessment, your loved one is assigned a case manager to determine the number of hours of care they are eligible to receive, based on their ability to move around. You will be lucky if your parent or loved one is eligible for more than two or three hours a day. Once the hours are determined, you must then search on your own to find an in-home care provider, and the IHSS issues payment to that provider based on the number of hours they work. If you don't like the number of the hours provided to your loved one under what is called Domestic Services, you can appeal and request a State Hearing, another long and bureaucratic process in itself.

The pay for the caregiver is minimum wage. In the state of California in 2009, then Governor Arnold Schwarzenegger cut millions of dollars from the IHSS budget and Governor Jerry Brown is now doing the same thing, causing hours to be broken down by related services per week, including meal preparation and cleanup, routine laundry, shopping for food, and other errands.

Finding a good caregiver who will work for minimum wage is next to impossible. This is what Medicare is offering as assistance? I tried multiple avenues to find that elusive caregiver. There are a number of services that recommend caregivers and, as you might guess, the level of competence is commensurate with the pay. Some of the people sent to me by various agencies were in worse shape than Mom. Two people that came to the house for an interview had no address and were apparently homeless. I finally put an ad in the Los Angeles Times to get help.

There are so many holes in the Medicare system they're too shameful to mention. When I interviewed people for the job of providing care for my Mom, most laughed when I mentioned the pay. Fortunately, my sister Theresa finally recommended Pearl, a woman she knew who had experience in caregiving. We filled out all of the paperwork, and I agreed to supplement what IHSS was paying. The problem with the bureaucracy is that the caregiver must wait four to six weeks to get paid. Most people are not willing or able to wait that long for a paycheck. As soon as Pearl received her first check, she resigned. I understood. Earning minimum wage for providing 20 hours of caregiving each week is simply not worth the work, explained to me by more than one caregiver. It was back to the drawing board for me. My belief system is that you either love working with seniors and/or disabled people, or the job is not for you.

The truth is, taking care of a parent or other loved one has a different dynamic than caring for another person—many people see that as just changing someone's dirty diapers. Good pay or not, it's hard work. The assistance that the federal government provides— Medicare—is largely a disappointment. The design of the program has been so mismanaged that some things are allowed to happen even though they should not. The reason Medicare is a farce is because you are led to believe that you are entitled to more than you actually are. Nevertheless, there are some people who find Medicare beneficial, in particular those who have secondary insurance and/or are affluent enough to afford the costs.

SORTING IT OUT

There are two primary parts to Medicare. *Medicare Part* A is listed as *Hospital Insurance* and covers your stay in the hospital or in a skilled nursing facility, both of which are under the umbrella of professional care. My experience is that many of them are not professionals, but that is another story. If you are in a hospice facility or are receiving your care at home, you're within the framework of *Part A*. The only problem with the benefit is that you have what is called a "Benefit Period," the two-month period you have been either in the hospital or receiving care at home. After that two-month period, Medicare stops paying and your deductible comes into play. If your loved one was in the hospital and then rushed out, when they probably needed to stay, it was likely due to the fact that the hospital was no longer being paid by Medicare and the $1,000 deductible became due. That amount varies according to amount of income. Medicare is insurance.

Part A also only pays for the hospital room, not all the medical services you are in the hospital to receive, and only a part of that. If you're there for the surgery, you can leave the hospital with a bill in the 10s and 1000s of dollars.

Medicare Part B is listed as *Medical Insurance* and covers some doctor services but not all. This is why at every doctor's appointment, it is important to note whether the visit will be paid for by Medicare. Part B will also cover medical equipment like a hospital bed for the home, grab bars, shower tables, and general supplies (such as bedside commodes, bedpans, etc.) Doctor-recommended services like X-rays and laboratory services for blood and urine tests are also included. Emergency ambulance service is covered as well, and they will generally take the patient to the nearest hospital for an emergency.

Part B has costs associated with it and is a voluntary program. You must meet the $1,000 deductible, after which Medicare will begin paying 80% of the bill. Your loved one's primary care physician should be helpful in assisting you with this part of Medicare. You will need supplemental insurance for any additional benefits, for which you are eligible only if your *Part B* premium is paid (it is then transferred to the private insurer), which millions of seniors can't afford.

For more detailed information on what Medicare does and does not cover, visit **www.Medicare.gov**. There is also a section of the website specifically for caregivers. See http://www.medicare.gov/ caregivers/.

If you peeled back the layers of Medicare, you would see that the lobbyists for the drug industry have done one fine job in making sure they profit from seniors. New Hampshire lawmakers learned an important lesson in 1981, when they limited the number of prescriptions that seniors could have filled. In 11 months, medication costs for seniors dropped 35%, but admissions to nursing homes shot up nearly 60%. When lawmakers removed the limitation, admissions returned to normal, and total health care costs declined. Those results served as further reason to keep the ban on importing prescription drugs from abroad.

Why would the U.S. allow its citizens to buy their medication from other countries, when they can make them buy the medication at home and everyone can split the enormous profits? Drugs from Canada would be allowed into the U.S. if the Department of Health and Human Services certified their safety. Are we surprised that the Department has yet to certify any, especially when one considers that prescription drugs in Canada are often sold for 1/10 of the cost they are sold for in the U.S.? Maybe the pharmaceutical companies are running the U.S. after all!

Another unpleasant part of the Medicare system is that the people they send to provide in-home assistance with actual care are, in most cases, Registered Nurses. The nurses come in and check the patient's vitals, spend a few minutes with them, and sometimes arrive at diagnoses that they aren't qualified to make. One of the nurses sent to check on Mom told me that she was ordering some medicine for Mom. I asked why, and her answer was that Mom had an infection. The young lady was confident and self-assured, and made the statement with conviction. I was a bit surprised that she could make that diagnosis without even a urine or blood sample. She became a little uncomfortable with my questioning, as though I were interfering with the natural order of things. It turned out that Mom didn't have an infection after all and did not need the medicine that the nurse ordered. This was confirmed by Mom's physician when she refused the request for the additional medicine. Once again, being vigilant paid off.

Medicare Part C includes Medicare Advantage plans, like health maintenance organizations (HMO's) and Preferred Provider Organizations (PPO's). These are managed care plans and other options from which Medicare beneficiaries may choose. Some plans charge a premium beyond the Part B premium the fed transfers to them.

Medicare Part D provides options for prescription drug coverage for everyone with Medicare. This coverage lowers prescription drug costs and protects against higher costs in the future. If you join a Medicare drug plan, you usually pay a monthly premium. If you do not opt for one of the plans (many can't afford to or don't have Part B), Medicare will assign you a provider that enables the cost of each prescription to be from $1-$3 as long as the medication is on Medicare's annual list of eligible pharmaceuticals. Many doctors and others authorized to write prescriptions will write them for a 3-6-month supply to reduce the cost to the patient even further. These plans are run by insurance companies and other private companies approved by Medicare.

The bottom line is that you have to pay for *Parts C and D*. You can read and research all you want, and that will not change the fact that there is a price to pay. When you include insurance companies and private companies, the writing is on the wall.

Read the fine print. When you reach the age of 65, Social Security will send you a red, white and blue card for Medicare. If you have decided to retire at 62, know that $100.00 will be deducted monthly from that check on your 65th birthday. Social Security will not ask you, they will just deduct it automatically from your check, many lower income people do not know they have a choice about this, but they will inform you of the change. If you have medical insurance from a retirement benefit or one that you have paid into—do your research.

WHAT IS THE DIFFERENCE BETWEEN MEDICARE AND MEDICAID?

As the cost of Medicare and the services it doesn't fully cover has risen dramatically in recent years, and the privatization of hospitals has eliminated "charity care" options from most, more and more seniors are having to rely on Medicaid to meet basic health care needs. Medicaid, however, is a state-run program that differs widely from state to state in terms of eligibility and limitations to coverage, but one can find out about individual states' requirements and content either online or by calling their local Social Services agency.

Here are some of the other differences:

Medicaid is for low-income:

• Pregnant women

- Children under the age of 19
- People 65 and over
- People who are blind
- People who are disabled
- People who need nursing home care

Application for Medicaid is at the State's Medicaid agency.

Medicare is for:

- People 65 and over
- People of any age who have kidney failure or long-term kidney disease
- People who are permanently disabled and cannot work

Medicare is automatically applied when the Social Security recipient reaches age 65.

HOSPICE CARE

Hospice Care service is end-of-life care provided by health professionals and volunteers. They give medical, psychological, and spiritual support. The goal of the care is to help people who are dying have peace, comfort, and dignity. The caregivers try to control pain and other symptoms so a person can remain as alert and comfortable as possible. Hospice programs also provide services to support a patient's family.

Usually, a hospice patient is expected to live six months or less. Hospice care can take place:

- At home
- At a hospice center
- In a hospital
- In a skilled nursing facility
- In an assisted living facility that offers it

How much does Hospice cost?

Because of volunteers, some services, like meals-on wheels, friendly visits, and telephone reassurance may be free or involve a low fee.

Generally, hospice costs less than hospital care, nursing homes, or other institutions due to help from insurance companies and government services.

Usually, the costs will only be for the services that the family cannot provide, but this may cost more when additional services or long-term and/or specialized care are needed.

When a patient age 65 or older is transferred to hospice, Medicare may help relieve some of the hospice care costs. Medicare coverage of hospice care is limited by time periods, and the patient may elect to receive hospice care for up to two periods of 90 days each, followed by an unlimited number of 60-day periods. A doctor must certify that the patient is terminally ill at the beginning of each care period.

HEALTH INSURANCE SUPPLEMENTS
NURSING HOME CARE

At some point in your caregiving, it may become necessary to consider using nursing home services. Nursing Homes serve as a permanent residence for people who are too frail or sick to live at home, or as a temporary facility during a recovering period. However, many people need a nursing home level of care but would prefer to remain in their own home with the help of their family and friends, community services, and professional care agencies. The Medicare program offers limited access to two unique programs for certain beneficiaries, who need a comprehensive medical and social service delivery system.

What does Medicare not cover?

- Dental care and dentures
- Routine foot care
- Cosmetic Surgery
- Experimental Procedures
- Personal comfort items, like a phone or TV in your hospital room
- Tests for and the cost of eyeglasses or hearing aids
- Services outside the United States (with certain exceptions)
- Most immunization shots (except flu and pneumonia shots which Part B helps pay)
- Custodial care—This is given by a medically unskilled person to help a patient with tasks of daily living, such as walking, bathing, or dressing. Even if you are in a hospital that participates in

Medicare or are in a skilled nursing facility, Medicare will not cover the cost of the service if it is mainly custodial
- Holistic Medicine (acupuncture, acupressure, chiropractors)

Understanding Social Security Benefits

In caring for a loved one, become knowledgeable about their benefits, including Social Security. Be aware that when you reach your full retirement age, you can work and earn as much as you want, and still receive your full social security benefit payment. If you are younger than full retirement age and if your earnings exceed certain dollar amounts, some of your benefit payments during the year will be withheld. Check with your local Social Security Office.

FULL RETIREMENT AGE

For persons born during the years 1943-1954, the full retirement age is 66. If you were not born in this period, you can research *www. socialsecurity.gov* for your statement.

RETIRING EARLY

If you earned 40 credits over your work life, you can start receiving Social Security benefits at 62 or at any month between 62 and full retirement age. However, your benefits will be reduced based on the number of months you receive benefits before reaching full retirement age.

If your full retirement age is 66, benefits will be reduced:
- 30% at age 62
- 25% at age 63
- 20% at age 64
- 13.3% at age 65
- 6.7% at age 66

Delaying Retirement

You may decide to wait beyond your full retirement age before choosing to receive benefits. If so, your benefit will be increased by a certain percentage for each month you don't receive benefits between your full retirement age and age 70.

Note that your cumulative benefits are higher the earlier you start, even though your monthly benefit starts higher the later you enroll.

OBAMACARE

Do you think insurance companies should be able to revoke coverage when someone gets sick? Or deny coverage because they have a pre-existing condition? I believe most people will say NO.

And that is good, because that's the first thing the Affordable Care Act does. It bans those outrageous insurance company practices. Since President Obama embraced the word "Obamacare," henceforth I will address it as such although some now call it "Bidencare." There are FIVE basic components to Obamacare:

- **Insurance Regulations**: It bans insurance companies from revolving or denying coverage because you get sick.
- **Subsidies**: It provides subsidies to make sure everyone under age 65 can afford to buy insurance.
- **Online Exchanges**: It establishes online exchanges where you can shop for insurance coverage unless you are over 65, in order to promote competition and keep companies honest.
- **Paying For the Act**: It pays for the subsidies with a combination of spending cuts and taxes on the companies that benefit from reform.

IN SUMMARY

The Medicare program is a federal health insurance program for people 65 years of age and older. There are four parts, each of which has its own requirements. Eligibility for Medicare means you are a U.S citizen or permanent resident with a work history able to receive the benefits of Social Security. You worked long enough in a "covered" job to be insured by Medicare. Obamacare prevents insurance companies from denying coverage from those who have pre-existing conditions, and that insurance is now affordable for individuals and families in the middle-income range. Medicaid is based on income and serves seniors who can't afford Medicare, in many states.

WISE TIPS

In order to take advantage of what Medicare has to offer you should have supplemental insurance if you can afford it. The American Association of Retired Persons (AARP) has one of the best hook-ups in the supplemental health insurance business. There are others that include many HMO's and PPO's for your selection, like Humana. You will be wise to enroll in these programs at the minute they are available if you can.

CAREGIVING QUOTES

To let pharmaceutical companies get away with paying nothing while poor and disabled people lose health coverage is unconscionable.

— CONGRESSMAN HENRY WAXMAN, Democrat, Beverly Hills, CA

The things you do for yourself are gone when you are gone, but the things you do for others remain as your legacy.

— KALU KALU

CHAPTER 11
Dealing with Burnout

"Lost time is never found again."
— THELONIUS MONK

WHEN YOU ARE taking care of someone by yourself, there is seldom time to rest or play. There is always something that needs to be done. Many caregivers work 24 hours a day, seven days a week, and all 365 days of the year. Rest is at a premium; naps are almost always unsettled; and sleep is generally in two-hour chunks—no weekends off, no vacations from the awesome responsibility of taking care of your loved one. It is an overwhelming responsibility with no reward at the end—and sometimes it seems that there is no end. I'm talking about "burnout." Burnout comes from all work and no play.

When you are a primary caregiver for a loved one, some of your friends and relatives won't understand or appreciate what you are going through. Even family members who won't participate in any of the caregiving will criticize the caregiver. As a rule, caregivers are not appreciated by those closest to them. And worse yet, your loved one may not recognize or respect the effort it takes to be on the premises with them around the clock. The caregiver is seldom going to get his or her due.

It doesn't take a rocket scientist to know that negative attitudes can add to the stress of the caregiver and to the feelings of isolation from spending hours on end being on call. It is only logical that if the caregiver is stressed, he or she will pass on some of what they are feeling to those around them. If civilized society is judged by how it treats its seniors, how then, do we judge how family treats its caregivers?

Often, when a parent is ill or elderly, they depend on their caregiver, not on the occasional visitor. The person who is there every day is the one making the sacrifice. Of course, mothers know how to play one child against the other by praising the infrequent visitor as the savior; s/he is the understanding and attentive one. It is not unusual for the primary caregiver to get none of the recognition s/he rightfully deserves.

At times, one family member may decide to criticize another family member for doing what others don't want to do. Since the family member has grown into the role of caregiver, the change from being cared for by one's mother to now caring for her is lost in translation (or transition). Unfortunately, animosity present within the family unit is not uncommon when the caregiver is stressed, taken for granted, and the communication between family members breaks down.

As discussed earlier, arranging for others to assist with daily tasks or to volunteer to plan activities would be one way to change the thinking process of the family and transform the whole situation into a win-win for everyone. Such respite care provides caregivers a temporary relief from burnout. It is designed to assist by having another person care for the loved one for a night or a weekend to give the caregiver some relief. It allows the caregiver to take time to relax, regroup, and come back rested and ready to provide good care again.

If you are a caregiver, look for solutions. Listen to some of what your friends have to say. Be open to suggestions from others, as they can see you differently than you may see yourself and will notice changes. If you can't recognize that you are suffering from burnout, you probably are not listening to your friends. Allow your family to help. You have resources, and they are all around you. If you are one of those people who can't move forward unless things are done perfectly, get a grip. You can't do it all alone.

Caregiving is a different ballgame. Manage your time and make some time for yourself. Meditate. Find a group that you can do Yoga with and your life will change. The exercise will slow you down after you've been running at a frantic pace. Unmanaged stress can bring about a lot of negative actions like drinking alcohol, smoking, and overeating, none of which are good. The end solution must be for you to take care of yourself, so that you can take care of your loved one.

Possible solution: Respite care would be one way to change the thinking process of the family and transform the whole situation into a win-win for everyone.

"We usually see things not as they are but as we are."
— LOUISE BEAVERS

Leanne's Story

Leanne had been the primary caregiver for her husband, Joseph Louis, for the last 10 years. She was the organizer and matriarch of her family. Her journey from wife to caregiver exemplifies the toll it takes to care for someone that you love. It is a familiar story shared by many.

Joe and I had been friends for over 25 years. He was introduced to me by my mentor and mutual friend, Whitman Mayo. Joe, the writer, community organizer, father, and intellectual, was a graduate of Rutgers University. He did with books what many people do with food—devour. His personality was what I call the "East Coast edge." Not necessarily rude, but very rough around the edges at editing his thoughts when communicating personally. And while many urbanites like Joe love the fact that they are viewed as having an edge, it is offensive to many. In Los Angeles, people will appear to be listening, when they're really just tuning you out as wasted time. An urbanite will tell you to get lost, rather than have a meaningless conversation: no time wasted. I like that about urbanites. What intensifies the edge is when that urbanite is 6'5" and weighs 300 pounds, has a full beard and wears an African dashiki. Without saying a word, Joe basically scared off half the people he came into contact with. In 10 minutes, Joe could suck the air out of a room. He loved that.

When I met him, Joe was having problems with his health. His family has a history of diabetes; his sister died from complications due to diabetes, and his older brother was also diabetic and barely able to walk at 69 years old. Joe, too, was diabetic and took insulin on a daily basis. The combination of family history, diet, and lifestyle were not working in his favor. Joe was a prime example of not sticking to the health regimen he needed to survive, and eventually physical and mental declines were rapid and dramatic.

Joe's declining health began taking its toll. In the first of his many surgeries, incisions were made on the insides of both of his legs, from the groin almost to the ankles, and this was life-changing. For the first time in Joe's adult life he could not walk on his own. He was wheelchair-bound.

The recovery had left Joe in a somber and sour mood, and his wife Leanne became his full-time caregiver, whether she wanted to be or not.

Leanne had been a practicing Buddhist for more than 20 years. Her mastery of the art of chanting for relaxation undoubtedly helped her cope with the stress, along with support from a wonderful group called the Well Spouse Association. Leanne was also dealing with an ailing father in Philadelphia, and a son who was having some rather difficult issues that he was finding hard to navigate. Her many roles evolved into Enabler, Matriarch, Mother, Daughter, Friend, Sister, Breadwinner, Wife, and Supervisor—all the ingredients needed for a classic burnout recipe.

At my last visit, Joe was being served like a king. His meals were brought to his side as he watched CNN, and he ate breakfast in bed if he so desired. The week-long visit was quite enlightening. Joe showed off the list of medications he was taking and how Leanne had them categorized. The brother was being well taken care of. One night while Joe was eating dinner, I noticed the extra salt he was adding to his food. I remarked on how harmful that additional salt was, and as usual, he had an answer. He smoked, even though he knew that it would only exacerbate his present condition. He would go through periods of exercising, only to stop and succumb to sweets. He knew all of the things that he should be doing yet continued to tempt his own fate with fundamentally poor decisions.

When Leanne first met Joe, he was working on a novel and running his own non-profit organization, Themebelutu, to assist inner city youth in Washington, D.C. When Themebelutu lost its funding, Joe's true passion was lost along with it. His depression did not help matters and his physical condition worsened. His diabetes reached a point where modern medicine could not stop the inevitable—more surgery.

He ended up having five toes removed—the big toe and small toe on the right foot, and three other toes on the left foot. Joe was really down.

Leanne kept me updated on Joe's condition, and from that communication I could see how being Joe's caregiver—along with all of her other roles—began to unravel her at the seams.

Emails from Leanne:

September 13, 2007

The laparoscopic surgery was totally successful. Joe's gall bladder had been swollen several times its normal size and was only functioning at 13% capacity. He is still in post-op pain, so tonight I will meet again with the doctors to see what the next steps are.

September 23, 2007

My father died overnight. I am staying in Philadelphia to help my brother prepare for the funeral later this week. Joe needs your support more than ever now. Doctors will CATscan him again sometime this week to be absolutely sure they have not missed anything. Thanks for everyone's prayers during such an extraordinarily difficult time.

October 9, 2007

We are about to hit the road. Discharge planning and transferring Joe to a sub-acute facility where he will get PT/OT and adequate medical supervision. The hospital case manager called today; she sounded a bit brisk, but only because she knows what the odds are against getting a good placement.

Kesha [Joe's youngest daughter] is still here, so she's keeping an eye on me. I am back at work today. My conference is exactly 30 days away and I will be getting directly in touch with the grantees, 90% of whom have yet to register, etc.

October 19, 2007

Joe still needs placement at a sub-acute facility that can give him adequate medical care and physical therapy. Twenty places contacted, they each have said no deal. I will try to reach the elder care lawyer who thinks he can get Joe qualified for Medicaid if we can get a facility to admit him. The deal: they want to know where the money is coming from after the insurance stops paying.

Due to extensive medications and as yet unspecified low-grade infections, he is frequently lethargic or agitated. If he comes home, I will negotiate for private-pay care. The hospital says they're discharging him either way on Monday.

November 18, 2007

Joe is still basically bedridden, with hand and forearm tremors, and getting weaker by the day due to lack of regular supervised activity (PT/OT, speech therapy and mental health). He is able to rally a bit in the morning to get his diaper changed, take his meds, be fed, get washed at the basin and dressed. Because the bed is adjustable and he is alert, getting him into the wheelchair is almost doable by midday.

By dinner he is not well-oriented, primarily because of pain. His appetite is slow. It is almost impossible to get him to transfer back into bed; last night it took three hours. We have called 911 three times in the past week for falls.

He has three follow-up appointments in the next month, each requiring almost a full day to transport, wait, and interview, in addition to his regular custodial care (diaper and clothing changes, medication management, and meal prep/ serve/ cleanup).

It is $350-500/week for a few hours of home nursing aide care—add $200 when I needed someone overnight while I was at a job-related meeting. I cannot continue.

The insurance company sent an occupational therapist and nurse after 3.5 weeks of promises on their part and begging on mine. They say they will send a paid home health aide, but that hasn't happened either.

Two different private referral services are looking for a nursing home, but so far, all have said his situation is too complicated for them.

I will be going to see my brother, daughter, and granddaughter on Thanksgiving, so I will get an aide to be with Joe overnight.

Joe does not have the support he needs. I need to know if and how you want to participate in his care, as I am unable to continue under these circumstances. I have no more paid leave or assigned leave hours until January 15, 2008.

From a month of sleeping in 2-3-hour spurts, I almost fell out of a chair in the middle of the National Science Research meeting for which I am responsible.

March 5, 2008

As you know by now, Joe was admitted to Washington Hospital Center on Sunday morning after more than 10 hours in the emergency room. His third toe has badly deteriorated over the past week, and Joe said the fourth toe hurt as much as the other one, which had swollen badly and turned dark like gangrene.

They only did ultrasounds last night and began antibiotics today in an attempt to save the toe, but they won't decide on treatment until they evaluate tissue cultures tomorrow.

Five years passed by, and it seemed as though Joe might never be able to walk again. Leanne continued to take care of Joe and tried to find him some help, but she often talked about "breaking free" and going out on her own. She was tired and beaten. She had taken more than just about any woman I know. She made the decision to leave her marriage and for the first time in 10 years, finally did feel "free." Not quite guilt-free though, as Joe had tried every maneuver available. He wanted to come home and live, but he couldn't walk. Leanne had to work and couldn't be home to take care of him. She made too much money for Medicare to relinquish any funds and the options were minimal. She had been in and out of hospitals with Joe for seven years—and for five of those years, Joe had not walked. He had been close to death a number of times. Joe was curt with staff and anyone else with whom he came in contact.

Leanne was at her wit's end because as Joe's legal wife and the head of the household she made too much money for Joe to be on welfare, but in the current arrangement she didn't make enough on which to live. With a six-figure income, she was barely scraping by—the hospital bills and medication costs had left her with nothing. She had to borrow money from friends and family just to get by.

The big decision was whether to bring Joe home. He had been in and out of the hospital for the last five years. He couldn't be left alone. He had lain on the floor for five hours more than once, because the caregiver was unable to lift him. He had resisted being in a caregiving facility and refused even to talk about it.

They reached a final step when Leanne finally found a place for Joe with everything necessary to rehabilitate and invigorate him. The night he was to be transferred from the hospital to the facility, he went ballistic on the staff and the doctors. The facility where he was supposed to go refused to allow him there under any circumstances. The hospital told Leanne that they were discharging Joe as soon as possible. Leanne had some tough decisions to make.

Kesha was in from New York and had power of attorney for him. She is, by profession, a practicing lawyer. Leanne had given up her two-bedroom apartment and was living in an efficiency. No room for Joe. All that he owned was in storage. His refusal to accept going to the nursing home and his discharge from the hospital had caused them all to stay in a hotel for the weekend.

There was nowhere else for Joe to go. The family conferred about what to do next. Joe took an overdose of his medication and was rushed to the hospital. He was in intensive care and no one knew quite what to do. When Joe recovered, Kesha and Leanne were at his side. But Joe did not want to live.

Leanne was back at work and receiving calls from Joe, telling her how low-down she was, another form of placing guilt. Leanne had been through hell.

Nevertheless, she began to feel empowered—she and Joe were separated, a divorce was pending, and she was no longer his caregiver—all of which made him eligible for coverage under Medicaid. Joe could get the treatment he needed. Kesha headed back to New York, and Joe decided that he would try the new care facility.

January 28, 2009

Please call Joe tomorrow because he is having a tooth pulled this afternoon. He will also move to a much better place by the end of the month. The place where he is, is very sad and not working in too many ways to detail. He spent two days last week in the city's homeless shelter for men (that's another story).

Things never seemed to come together for Joe. His health continued to decline and all of his resources had been exhausted. In May of 2009 Joe passed away in a Washington, D.C. motel room. Leanne had a service for him at the Buddhist Temple in D.C.. All four of Joe's daughters were in attendance. Leanne's relief was evident, without words.

TIPS FOR FAMILY CAREGIVERS

- Watch out for signs of depression, and don't delay in getting professional help.
- Be willing to accept help from other people—have assignments for them to perform. Share the care.
- Caregiving is a job and respite is your earned right. Reward yourself—take a break.
- Watch out for the heavy lifting, pushing and pulling—be good to your back.
- Trust your instincts. Reach out to your network for some of the answers and help.

IN SUMMARY

It will take everything that you have to care for a loved one. That is a fact. It will take equally as much for you to take care of yourself, if you are the primary caregiver. Finding time for yourself is impera-tive—exercise, meet with friends, carve out time for yourself by any means.

WISE TIPS

Respite simply means getting a break from your caregiving responsibilities for a few hours or a few days. It will not eliminate all of your problems, but it certainly will make you feel better.

"We usually see things not as they are but as we are."

— LOUISE BEAVERS

CHAPTER 12
Death and Dying

"Hold no man responsible for what he says in grief.
— Talmud

IN THE MIDST of our caregiving, it is not unusual to put off planning for the inevitable.

Many families cremate their loved one's remains and still have a funeral, renting a casket for the visitation service.

PLAN AHEAD

We are all reluctant to talk about death. It's almost like, if you don't talk about it won't happen, but we all know better. In many cases, even as Mom or Dad is dying, the family drags its feet. And only when the reality of the death is upon them do they scramble among family and friends to find a funeral home. The advantage of planning is that you are able to choose the type of funeral home and service you want, so it is not left up to the funeral home or the survivors to try and figure it out.

It is best to look into your options now. Visit some of the funeral homes while you can make a wise decision. When you are dealing with the stress and emotions from a loved one's death, it is hard to think rationally. And time being of the essence, your judgment is generally not "state of the art." Remember that those funeral homes thrive on bereavement. They know that the grief, disbelief, sadness, and numbness are a part of your decision-making process. Talk to them and let them know you are weighing your options, doing some comparative shopping, and making decisions that are wise and prudent.

Whichever way you decide to go, it makes sense to look at all of the options.

Some funeral homes in the community have been around for a very long time. However, in today's marketplace it is hard to know whether the funeral home will be around when you or your loved one dies. Some funeral homes go out of business pretty fast. In some cases, they are bought by other funeral homes. Think about what happens if you move. Does the funeral plan go with you? A lot of people have already invested in funeral services that they may not ever be able to use. An estimated 12 million Americans have spent over $22 billion on pre-paid funeral arrangements.

If you are pre-paying for yourself, make sure that two members of your family have copies of the paperwork. They should be family members, whom you know will be the ones to follow up on the contracts to see that they are fulfilled. They will have the information about who is to be called to make arrangements, and answers to questions like: Where will the viewing or "wake" take place? Are the prices locked in, or can they be changed? What are the provisions if you should be out of the local area or state at the time of death?

One of the great things about doing this is that it is not necessary to prepay.

Shop around before you settle on anything. It is recommended that you compare at least three places, because you will find that prices can vary dramatically. Find out what is and is not included in the price. Going online to compare prices from funeral homes and crematoriums can save you a ton of money. Even warehouse shopping clubs like Costco sell caskets now. The Funeral Consumers Alliance (FCA) produces a booklet called "Before I Go, You Should Know," which is also quite helpful.

I once managed a call center for an organization called the Neptune Society, which specializes in cremation. My employees were given a list of names to call and set up appointments for the salesmen to go and convince clients to have their body, or the body of a loved one, cremated on that inevitable day. The responses were varied. Most of the people didn't want to think about it. Many of the people said that they would not worry about it until that time came. Some said that cremation was against their beliefs, that one should be buried with a funeral service.

The truth is that once the life is gone, the body deteriorates pretty fast. As a matter of fact, the gruesome truth is that the fluids used to embalm the body eventually seep to the bottom of the casket. Traditional burial is an old ritual and is no longer the only option.

Around the United States, cremation is becoming more and more the norm. In many parts of the world, like Canada, half of the people there are cremated. In Japan the rate of cremation is closer to 90%. One of the biggest advantages of cremation is that it is less expensive than a funeral and a cemetery burial. No embalming, no gravesite, no casket, and no salesman trying to sell you things based on guilt and grief is involved. The Neptune Society prices for cremation are at the high end. You receive an urn and the guarantee of one price for $1,700, which is premium in the business. Check with the average funeral home and you'll find the cost of cremation to be anywhere from $500 to $700 for everything. But beware!

Funeral homes prey on grief-stricken family members. They know how to up-sell you to buy and spend what you don't have. It's their business, and they spend a lot of time learning the nuances of selling.

I can hear people now saying that it is wrong to cremate, and it's not what their mother wants. My experience with my people— black folk—is that we are going to "do it up." Give us the best casket and service and burial plot. We are going to send Mama off in style, and to do anything less is sacrilegious.

A friend's mother died a few years ago and he had to borrow money to bury her. He had an elaborate service for her but didn't even have a job, nor did anyone in his family at that time. Avoid the money pitfall that has become a part of death and dying.

Don't procrastinate; plan ahead.

PHENOMENAL WOMAN

In November of 2007 I flew to Memphis to meet up with my sister Stephanie and brother-in-law, Larry. Larry's mom had just passed away at the age of 89 after a long illness.

I arrived on a Monday night and made my bed on Linda Gayle's couch. Linda is one of Larry's sisters and was also one of Mother Josie's primary caregivers. We all stayed up late into the night discussing the arrangements for the funeral, which were being held about 70 miles south of Memphis in Helena, Arkansas—hometown to "Mother Josie," as she was affectionately called, Larry, and five of his siblings.

We looked over the obituary and talked about the program. Linda had been running things since Mother Josie made the move from Helena to Memphis, when she could no longer live by herself. During the later stage of her life, Mother Josie suffered from dementia. She knew Larry's face, but didn't know his name. Realizing that your own mother doesn't recognize you is always somewhat of a shock.

We discussed accommodations for everyone who was coming from out of town for the funeral. Everyone was pitching in with ideas and thoughts about what to do. Larry has a total of five sisters, so everything that needed to be done had been done, or soon would be. I was just there for support.

Events took over. It was three o'clock in the morning, and only then were heads beginning to hit the pillow. I was on Los Angeles time—for me it was only midnight—but I forced myself to close my eyes and began to feel the pain of sharing the loss of a loved one. It had been 10 years since Mom died at Brotman.

The next morning was hectic. A lot of things had to be done. We piled into two cars and drove to the airport to pick up Eboni, Stephanie's daughter, who was flying in from Maryland with her two youngest children. We all caravanned to the hotel, where most of the family was staying. We were in Mississippi, two miles across the bridge from Helena. We checked into our block of rooms, went to the church to place flowers, returned to the hotel to change clothes, and then drove back to the church for the wake. Afterward was a family dinner, where we gathered and remembered Mother Josie's love and impact of her spirit on Helena, Arkansas.

The funeral service took place on Wednesday afternoon at a larger church, with people who had come to remember Mother Josie. The choir consisted of eight women, and I am certain no one singing in that choir was under the age of 70. I felt at home. I am touched by the South, particularly the rural South.

Linda Gayle delivered the eulogy; she rocked the house. Her message combined the late Maya Angelou's "Phenomenal Woman" with her own words.

The Minister was old school; he preached with the rhythm of song and from time to time his head would go back and forth, as if he were reaching for something extra. He was incredible, and his words lingered in the church, along with choruses of "amen" to let him know we were with him. He occasionally paused for effect to wipe his brow with a large, white handkerchief. The service was truly inspirational.

"Dying is a very dull and dreary affair. And my advice to you is to have nothing to do with it."

— William S. Maugham

FLYING HOME

The experience of Mother Josie's funeral caused me to recall my own mother's death. Three days before Mom died, I went to the hospital to visit her. After seeing her lying there almost lifeless, I went home and cried all night. I couldn't stop crying. I was unable to go back to the hospital again after that. I called my friend Judge and told him my story, and he assured me that it was okay. After a long silence, I told Judge that I would call him back. I hung up, because the emotion of the moment was too much to express. I called him back a couple of hours later, still feeling raw with emotion and said, "I'm trying to get it together." Judge interrupted and said, "It's alright, Butch, you did the job you were supposed to do. You don't have to go back to the hospital." Those were the exact words I needed at the time. I just laid on the bed in complete exhaustion. I didn't go back to the hospital, and Mom died three days later.

Dr. Taylor phoned me with the news, and I called Judge and Jon. They both came over and sat with me. We drank wine and talked. I was in space. As a matter of fact, I couldn't do anything else. I left everything to my sisters. They made all of the funeral arrangements and let everyone know that Mom had made her trip to heaven. I barely talked that whole week.

At the funeral, I was with friends and family. I sat in the pew with my shades on, like I was hiding. I was drained and seemed to be somewhere else. I heard everyone speak at the funeral. It was inspiring. But I didn't cry. I saw Mom in her casket and bent down to kiss her cheek. I returned to the pew and didn't move until we left the church to go to the burial.

Family was there, giving their love. One of my dear friends and tennis partners, Lloyd Ferguson, was there and whispered in my ear: "We are proud of you, Butch." That made me feel good. Sometimes you don't realize that people are watching—but they are. I barely noticed Mom's baby brother at the service, until Joe Louis elbowed me in the side and asked, "Is that Illinois Jacquet?" I looked up and there he was. I nodded, acknowledging his presence and hugged him on the way out of the church. I thanked him for the financial assistance with Mom's care. His gesture had made things a lot easier than they otherwise would have been. I didn't do anything for another whole week. No crying, only reflecting. Mom was home—she got her wings and flew home.

IN SUMMARY

Losing that someone special is never pleasant. Having family and friends is a blessing and allows us to deal with the grief. There is help out there to assist with bereavement counseling. Your minister, priest, or spiritual advisor should have an idea how you want to be cared for, which will help you work through a lot of the issues you face with the death of loved ones.

WISE TIP

Get your loved one's affairs in order prior to an actual death, and for yourself, appoint someone you trust, who will follow up on your final wishes. A living will allows you to document everything you want done, until the end.

"Death is not the end for someone who has faith."
— DESMOND TUTU

THE TEN COMMANDMENTS FOR SENIORS

I.   THOU SHALT NOT GIVE CREDIT CARD INFORMATON OVER THE PHONE.

More scams are out there than you can imagine. A rule of thumb: there are no free lunches. If you hear the word free hang up. You will hear of great prizes; just pay for the cost of shipping. You will also hear buzz-words like fantastic, spectacular, once in a lifetime opportunity, or no-risk opportunity. They are all lies, and I know from firsthand experience. There is a Do Not Call Registry—call toll free 1-888-382-1222. It will block your number from being called by telemarketers, at least the ones that subscribe to that list.

II.   THOU SHALT NOT TAKE COLLECT CALLS FROM ANYONE.

In this day and age, if the person can't make a call and pay for it, you don't need to accept it. Scammers will make long distance calls using your connection.

III.   THOU SHALT ASK QUESTIONS OF ALL DOCTORS, NURSES, AND CARE PROVIDERS.

It does not matter how silly you think the questions are— ask. Seniors are responsible for changing the world.

IV.   THOU SHALT ALWAYS ASK FOR A SECOND OPINION ON ANY INVASIVE SURGERY.

Think of your body as a fine-tuned car—you know from experience that some mechanics are good and some are horrible. If someone is going to cut on you—get a second opinion. Research. Ask another doctor, if you feel uncomfortable asking questions to your physician.

V.   THOU SHALT NOT LEAVE THE PLANET WITHOUT LEAVING A WILL.

If you die without a will, the state can step in—does not matter whether you have a lot of money or not. More than half the people over fifty don't have a will. If you don't have a lot of assets, you can go online and do it yourself.

VI. THOU SHALT LEARN TO ACCESS THE INTERNET.

You can go to a library, community college, high school, or university to learn the basics of a personal computer. Grandchildren can be your number one resource. They don't even know what typewriters are. Have them walk you through the process. They can print out the information from www.familydoctor.org. Seniors 65 and over are the fastest growing users of the internet. Get on board.

VII. THOU SHALT RESPECT THE PERSON TAKING CARE OF YOU.

Sometimes seniors get stuck in "I am still the boss" gear. My dear friend Joe never caught on to it. He could no longer walk yet he was ordering people around. It's bad enough that some people with money maintain that attitude. Once you reach the age where someone is taking care of you, be grateful. It is hard for some. Be nice.

VIII. THOU SHALT HAVE SOME ACTIVITY, GOAL OR AMBITION THAT WILL KEEP YOU BUSY FOR LIFE.

IX. THOU SHALT ASK THE FAMILY FOR HELP IN CARING FOR A LOVED ONE.

It is too easy to try and do it on your own. There is a lot of help out there, just ask. The small things make a difference.

X. THOU SHALT GIVE THIS BOOK TO FRIENDS AND FAMILY AND READ IT YOURSELF.

CHARTS AND CHECKLISTS

CHART 1

Name of Patient: _____

Medical Record Number: _____

List of Medications

Medication: _____

Prescription: _____

Non-Prescription RX# Unit Dosage Frequency Comments:

Medication:_____

Prescription:_____

Non-Prescription RX# Unit Dosage Frequency Comments:

CHART 2

Healthcare Contacts

Name:_____

Relationship to Patient:_____

Phone Numbers:

     Home:_____

     Work:_____

Comments:_____

Name:_____

Relationship to Patient: _____

Phone Numbers:

     Home:_____

     Work:_____

Comments:_____

SICK ROOM CHECK LIST

Item	Status Done
Hospital Bed	_____
Bedside Commode	_____
Pillows	_____
Sheets and Mattress Pad	_____
Foot Rest	_____
Cane	_____
Walker	_____
TV Trays	_____
Green Plant	_____
Urinals	_____
Trash Can	_____
Bottled Water	_____
Plastic Runner	_____
Neck Rest	_____
List of Medications	_____
Daily Pill Container	_____
Key Contact Numbers	_____
Underwear/Socks	_____
Bathing Supplies	_____
Books	_____
Reading Light	_____
Calendar	_____
Scratch Pads	_____
Post-A-Note	_____
Telephone	_____
Cell Phone	_____
Television	_____
CD Player	_____
Side Chairs for Guests	_____
Intercom	_____
Paper Towels	_____
Kleenex	_____
Pictures of Family	_____